WHEN IT'S NEVER ENOUGH

Daily Reflections of a Work Addict

Alexia H.

Cover designed by Madeline Baum

Alexia H.
Please feel free to let me know any feedback you have about this book, including editing comments, at alexiahaddictionrecovery@gmail.com For more information, check out www.activityaddiction.com. There may or may not be a website up. Because that, my friend, is how I roll in work addiction recovery.

Printed in the United States of America

First Printing: April 2018
Independently Published

ISBN 978-1-9807-2498-8

Forward

I have been in recovery from addictions for thirteen years, and specifically work and activity addiction for nine years. Many of the reflections on the following pages directly relate to the behaviors of workaholism, but many are insights I gleaned from recovery in general. I included them here because I believe these underlying causes and conditions cause me to act out in specific addictive behaviors. If I can find relief for the underlying issues, then I often don't need the escape of acting out through any of my addictions.

The entries are not in chronological order. They might be from early recovery or from last month. Thus, you'll note sometimes my children are living with me and other times not, and I may be at one job or another. I hope the lessons are relevant in your journey, regardless of where I am in mine.

I don't claim any of the ideas in the pages ahead are original to me. You may recognize many of the words of wisdom from the rooms of recovery. My goal was to mix these thoughts with my unique experiences in a way that might be useful to people suffering from workaholism.

How do you write a book about workaholism and do it soberly? Writing this book has been an opportunity to further apply recovery principles. I began writing in January of the first year and gave myself two years to complete it at a sober pace, writing one entry every two days. After the first four months, I began to panic that I was out of material. How could I possibly come up with 365 entries? Then it occurred to me the entries weren't something I could envision four months into the project. I needed to live my way through the book, using lessons I observed in June and September and December that weren't yet apparent to me in April. One day at a time, one entry at a time, I chose not to get ahead of myself.

Alexia H., April 2018

It always seems impossible until it is done. —Nelson Mandela

Contents

And the cat's in the cradle and the silver spoon
Little boy blue and the man in the moon
When you coming home, dad?
I don't know when
But we'll get together then
You know we'll have a good time then.
—Harry Chapin

Beth, I hear you calling
But I can't come home right now
Me and the boys are playing
And we just can't find the sound
Just a few more hours
And I'll be right home to you
I think I hear them calling
Oh Beth what can I do?
Beth what can I do?
— Stan Penridge, Peter Criss,
Bob Ezrin

January

For as long as I can recall, accomplishment was my priority. I was always a straight A student. Honor roll, Dean's list, law school, Masters degree, election to boards, speaking engagements, chairing conferences, working my way up the corporate ladder, finally being made a partner at one of the world's largest law firms. All of this makes me swell with pride. These are the achievements that earned me praise. Admiration and respect from others is a drug for me.

I took a year off between high school and college by graduating after my junior year. I worked three jobs to save money to go to Israel to visit my sister. When I was there for two months, I didn't have the work reward giving me the payoff I'd come to need, so I acted out in other ways, using alcohol, food and boys.

I would rather be working or talking about work than anything else in my life. I'm ashamed of this behavior and don't want my family to realize it. I wore out my sisters, husband, and friends talking about work.

I worry obsessively, about work problems in particular. For many years, I would pass out from drinking around 9:30 pm, and wake up at 2 am, concerned with a work problem and then be unable to fall asleep. My solution before recovery was to become addicted to Sominex, which I took every night for five years.

I am not a good delegator. I'm afraid that other people won't do it right. It often doesn't occur to me to delegate—I just assume that I need to do it all. This leaves me tired and resentful.

I suffer from perfectionism and I don't know how to let myself not know everything and be a beginner.

I have discomfort with vacations and returning from them was a nightmare. I check my messages at every lull in the action because I can't just *be*. I don't enjoy baths, sitting in a jacuzzi with my husband, walking the dog, hanging with my two kids and playing games. I force myself to walk the dog as long as I'm clocking aerobic minutes on my pedometer so I can meet my daily exercise goal.

I am obsessive about my lists.

I over-commit. I was a Girl Scout leader, and on a national committee for one of my 12-Step programs. I was on the committee to plan my 30th grade school reunion. I had a service position at each of my four weekly 12-Step meetings. I maintained an alumni list from one of my former employers and organized periodic lunches. I sponsored six women. I felt powerless to resign from any of these because I believed the work would not get done if I didn't do it or I would be letting people down.

I think strength training exercise each week is a good idea, but I can't seem to fit it into my schedule.

I don't have much of a sense of humor.

I fear that my obsessive activities prevent me from being available to hear God's will for me.

The Solution   January 2

I came into the rooms of Workaholics Anonymous (WA) and my life began to change. I attended meetings, found a sponsor, took suggestions that didn't make sense. I adopted bottom lines to define my sobriety and aimed at top lines to help ensure my balance. I worked the 12 Steps and began sponsoring people. I got healthy with food and exercise. I learned how to prioritize and have a daily action plan. I no longer need to be busy every minute. I pray and meditate daily. I get enough sleep. I get medical and dental attention when needed. I try not to multitask. I go to the bathroom when I need to, instead of trying to jam in just one more thing. I am grateful. I don't obsess about work as much. These are a small general taste of what has helped me in recovery. I have detailed more on the pages that follow.

Work Addiction   January 3

Despite being of above average intelligence, I suffered from low self-esteem. The two are seemingly unrelated. I often overcompensated for my perceived inadequacy by working harder. I got straight As in school. I needed to be a superstar at work; I craved recognition. I got three degrees and became a partner at a huge international law firm. I sat on boards. With each new accomplishment, after the accolades died down, the inevitable disillusionment followed: is this all there is? This wasn't so hard. Anyone could have done this. And the insatiable ambition kicked in again. More. That's what I needed.

10th Step Journal Entry   January 4

"An amazing day. This was the first day back to work after two weeks off for Christmas vacation. I aimed to do it soberly, and I did. I meditated in the morning. I told myself I didn't have to get everything done. I wrote my action plan and stuck to it. I did every priority task. I didn't let the email backlog make me crazy. I *enjoyed* my day. I went to the bathroom when needed and I got coffee. I took a break at 11:45 to say a prayer. I ate my lunch without multitasking, for half an hour. I read for fun on the train, instead of working. I let God shoulder the burden of anxiety and I did what was in front of me."

Scrupulosity   January 5

Scrupulosity is pathological guilt regarding moral or religious issues. It is personally distressing, objectively dysfunctional, and often accompanied by significant impairment in social functioning. It is typically a moral or religious form of obsessive-compulsive disorder. The term derives from the Latin *scrupulum*, a sharp stone, implying a stabbing pain on the conscience.

I was first introduced to this term at Workaholics Anonymous meetings. I could relate to it. Scrupulosity brought to mind the scene in *DaVinci Code* where Silas, the albino monk, a devotee of the Catholic organization Opus Dei, practices severe corporal mortification by flogging himself over a perceived shortcoming. My work addict carries a figurative whip. I am decidedly harsher on myself than on my staff. For instance, I used to make myself wait to go to the bathroom—just one more task, and then one more—until I was about to burst. One of my bottom lines today is to go to the bathroom as soon as I feel the urge. This is much healthier for my mind and body because it literally relieves the pressure.

I am also similar to Silas because I punish myself for making mistakes. My addict practices SHAME: Should Have Already Mastered Everything. As I now see it, this is my ego. Whereas other people get an opportunity to learn how to do things they never did before, I'm supposed to know how to do everything, intuit all the answers, without training or experience to guide me. When I remind myself that it is ok to make mistakes, that I get an opportunity to learn, that I'm no better or worse than anyone else, then I have a chance to stop practicing scrupulosity.

Finally, I'm similar to Silas in that I sometimes get rigid in following my recovery program. While it is optimal to set up structure including meetings, prayer and meditation, step work, sponsors, sponsees, and many other tools, I need to be alert regarding perfectionistic tendencies.

Recovery is supposed to give me a life, not be my life. — AA slogan

Illusion of Control   January 6

At work, I experience a cause-and-effect dynamic providing a "payoff" of the illusion of control. I get a sense of satisfaction and well-being from a job completed—I can make things happen at work. This payoff is a drug for me and I want more and more of it. The drug makes me feel good and valuable. Somebody asks me to do something. I do it. They are happy. I imagine they admire me. That gives me a dose of borrowed self-esteem. When things don't go well, the opposite happens. Someone is unhappy with me. I imagine they think I'm an idiot. I internalize that and believe I'm inadequate. What I need to focus on is whether my actions were God's will for me. As long as I'm doing God's will, other peoples' opinions are irrelevant.

Activity Chart   January 7

In early recovery before I got a sponsor, I found an exercise in the back of the Workaholics Anonymous Book of Recovery which proposes creating an activity chart and logging how I spent my time every day, in fifteen-minute increments. So, I set up the chart and kept track for six weeks. I knew what the numbers would show: I wasted time somewhere and I don't spend adequate time at my work, on my recovery or with my family. Going into the exercise I had a pervasive sense I was failing at everything.

But the results surprised me. Everything seemed to be in balance and I was doing the best I could do within the constraints of 24 hours a day. What a huge relief. It meant that my problem was one of perception. I wasn't failing, I simply *saw* myself as failing, and so changing my perception was where I needed to focus my efforts.

Signs of Surrender January 8

- When I try to stay present.
- When I have a sense of humor about how bad everything is going and what else could go wrong.
- When I sleep, trusting all will be well, even when momentous things are going on.
- When I get up from my computer when I'm very busy and walk to the bathroom or kitchen to clear my mind.
- When I refrain from sending an email with a negative message, and instead seek to speak to the person by phone or in person, even when inconvenient for me or when I have to be patient and not get immediate satisfaction.
- When I'm impatient, and I remind myself this is how long it takes for this thing to happen (computer to boot, doctor's visit, etc.) and I remind myself acceptance is the key to peace for me.

Character Defects January 9

My sponsor directed me to make a list of my shortcomings based on my 4th step work. Then I wrote how the defect manifested in my life, examples of it. I then identified the opposite of that defect, and how it might manifest in my life. My sponsor told me to meditate about each shortcoming and ask God for feedback. That meditation stands out in my mind as the most connected to HP I have ever felt.

As I considered my shortcomings and listened to God's input, I feel as though I channeled HP right into my laptop and captured his words. I'm pleased to say my Higher Power has a sense of humor. For instance, in response to my character defect of seeking approval from other people and people pleasing even at the expense of my needs, God said "Atta girl; you rock."

My list of defects also came into play on my 10th step. I ask myself the questions outlined in the AA Big Book, as well as questions customized to my shortcomings:
- what did I do for my husband today?
- What did I do for fun/inactivity?
- Where did I challenge myself to do something scary and outside of my comfort zone (a good thing)?
- Where did I avoid something I was afraid of (a bad thing)?
- Did I stand up for myself appropriately when needed?

6

Boundaries January 10

Last week, one of my partner's clients got sued. I've been working closely with my partner, Nancy, on the lawsuit. We tried to set up a meeting with one of the firm litigators, Joan, but the call kept getting delayed. Finally, we settled on 5pm on Monday night. I had indicated availability only until 6 pm.

My 6pm appointment was an exercise class, but I didn't need to share this with my partners. In the late afternoon, Joan advised us of a flight delay and her consequent inability to make the 5 pm call. Nancy emailed we *really* needed to meet and asked if we could do the call later in the evening. I reminded her of my availability, and the client indicated he wasn't particularly concerned with our delay. I tried calling Nancy at 5:25, but she texted she was talking to Joan and would call me in a minute.

At 5:40, I decided to leave for my class. I knew if I picked up the phone when Nancy called, I would not be able to gracefully end the discussion by 6 pm. When she called twice in the next ten minutes, I let it go to voicemail. I picked up the message at the gym and emailed back to the team that their plan for meeting the next day sounded great.

And it was great:
- the client was pleased when we met with him on Tuesday;
- I honored my boundary even though I struggled to enforce it; and
- I taught my partners I wouldn't let them walk on my boundaries for no real emergency.

Affirmations January 11

An affirmation is a short positive statement about an aspect of myself that I don't necessarily believe to be true, but I would like it to be. In fact, it may be exactly the opposite of what the tapes in my head tell me. When I first came into recovery, I thought affirmations were the stupidest, touchy feely thing I had ever heard. I couldn't imagine ever using them or how they would possibly make any difference.

After I completed my 6th step list of character defects, my sponsor directed me to develop one affirmation for each shortcoming. By the time I got to this place in my recovery, I was willing to be open enough to at least try to write the words. Then my sponsor suggested that I leave myself a voicemail message, saying each affirmation out loud. And then to periodically listen to them.

I recorded them in the second person, so when I listen to them, I imagine my Higher Power saying them to me ("You are enough" "You can set priorities and attend to tasks in a reasonable time frame"). It's like a shot in the arm whenever I am lacking confidence or feeling overwhelmed. I use specific affirmations when I'm confronted with the shortcoming, like when I have to speak in front of a group ("I am articulate and have important things to say").

Underscheduling   January 12

The practice of routinely "underscheduling" restores sanity to my life by giving me time to breathe and relax and interact playfully with other people in my life, instead of always being on task. For example:
-   9-10 Meeting
-   10-10:30 Unscheduled
-   10:30-11 Meeting
-   11-12 Paperwork
-   12-12:30 Lunch
-   12:30-2 Project
-   2-2:15 Unscheduled
-   2:15-3 Meeting
-   3-4 Work
-   4-5 Meeting

This tool allows me more peace of mind because it helps make up for activities that take longer than expected and provides a buffer between a tightly run schedule and total disarray and stress if things don't happen as planned.

'Cause you can't jump the track, we're like cars on a cable
And life's like an hourglass, glued to the table
No one can find the rewind button girl,
So cradle your head in your hands
And breathe, just breathe,
Whoa breathe, just breathe" —Anna Nalick

Powerlessness

I'm powerless over my work, activity and media addiction and my life has become unmanageable. I'm powerless over my ambition for power. For as long as I can recall, accomplishment was my priority. I have been working since grade school. I'm defined by my job--it is my identity. I have lots of energy around work. Most of the drama in my life has been about work—people I didn't get along with, fears about not being good enough. I'm powerless over work obsession and expect to be fired at any moment, even though things actually seem to be going well.

I am powerless over my default to do everything myself instead of asking for help or delegating. I'm powerless over my perfectionism. I fear that I will look stupid, particularly if the project involves speaking in front of others.

I had no trouble seeing my powerlessness and unmanageability over other addictions, but work addiction diagnosis is elusive. Our culture tells me to keep working harder, keep accomplishing the next objective. This makes denial easy. Even other 12-Step programs tell me to never say no when asked to serve.

I'm powerless over my inability to relax and play. I get restless, irritable and discontent. I think "what is the point?" There's no objective. No quantifiable work product.

I'm powerless over my lists. I'm powerless over my email inbox. I suffer from anxiety when there's too much in it. I have to respond to each inquiry or problem and can't prioritize. I lose hours responding to emails, when I should be focusing first on getting my daily goals for my job done.

I'm powerless over time, I'm constantly fighting a battle with the clock, not enough hours in the day to accomplish all of my commitments. I'm doing everything half-assed. I'm powerless over taking myself too seriously.

Top Lines

For many workaholics, abstinence means far more than relief from compulsive working and activity on a physical level. It also means an attitude that comes as a result of surrendering to something greater than the self. We do not merely avoid work, mistaking a lack of activity for recovery. We aspire to freedom from compulsive thinking and worrying. Each of us is free to determine our own way of being abstinent according to personal needs and preferences. Top lines represent our goals and visions... We work with a sponsor to establish such boundaries as well as to seek support around bottom line behavior. —The Workaholics Anonymous Book of Recovery, 2nd Edition.

Even though I'm powerless over my work addiction, I'm not helpless. There is a solution. It's made up of lots of different pieces — top lines which are quite different from the way I'm hard-wired. Here are some examples:

- I try to always have a fiction book that I'm reading, even though it is just for fun and doesn't accomplish a goal.
- I try to ask myself my motivation when I'm reaching for my phone to check for a text or email. Is it just to fill up a quiet moment with more stimulation?
- When I find myself worrying about my job during evenings or weekends, I remind myself that certain topics belong to work hours. I try to turn my attention to something else. Often, I meditate, and this clears my head of the problem.
- I encourage myself to go to bed at 9:30 most nights, because I know that rest is necessary for me to function the way God wants me to.
- I keep track of my work hours because I often get distracted by personal tasks and then shortchange my office. This keeps me clear about how much I'm actually working. My disease prefers vagueness.
- I pray and meditate almost every morning and evening. I ask God to give me direction about his will when I'm struggling with a particular problem.
- I try not to multitask.
- Before, I would not make time for meals because I was too busy, and then I would binge at night when my adrenaline level dropped. Today, I eat my meals at scheduled times, instead of letting it go until I'm starving.
- When I catch myself at work getting stressed or having a sense of urgency, I get up and walk around. Sometimes,

when I slow down, a creative solution to my problem appears effortlessly. Working smarter and not harder.
- I try to remind myself to enjoy the moment, particularly when I'm feeling bored. I try to find something about it for which I feel grateful.
- I used to race for the train, trying to make extremely tight time tables, trying to fit one more task in before the train. Now when I see that the next scheduled train will not allow me a leisurely pace, I readjust and aim for the next train instead. I often arrive early for the train so I can fit in a 10 minute walk around the neighborhood of the station before I get to the station.
- I take vacations and I enjoy them.

Bottom Lines   January 15

Bottom lines define the point where we cross over from abstinence to work addiction. –The Workaholics Anonymous Book of Recovery, 2nd Edition.

Bottom lines are compulsive behaviors I try to avoid. An example of a bottom line is "I don't work more than 45 hours a week at my professional job."

I don't have an abstinence date for my workaholism based on my bottom lines. I count my abstinence from the day I first came into work addiction recovery. If my abstinence date depended on my bottom lines, I could never cross those bottom lines, similar to AA where one never has another drink of alcohol. That is not a workable system for me in my work addiction. My addiction consists of many small behaviors amounting to a mountain of disease.

For instance, some of my bottom lines are: "not rushing," "go to the bathroom when I first feel the urge, and not try to fit in one more activity," and "not think about work more than one hour a week outside of work hours." I have around 50 of these. I get most of them right 95% of the time, but I don't do any of them perfectly. If my abstinence date depended on one of them, I would be resetting it often. That wouldn't be useful to me, or to newcomers who would conclude nobody could achieve more than five minutes of sobriety. My life is immeasurably better because of my imperfect abstinence. 95% is good enough, and further proves this is a program of progress, not perfection.

All Dressed Up and No Place to Go   January 16

The plan for today was to get packed up and drive to St. Louis to see a show my son was assistant directing. To that end, I got up early to address work projects, so I could then pack and drive five hours with my family. Over the course of the day, several people mentioned an ice storm in St. Louis. By 1 pm, I was ready to go and I started getting nervous and looked into the weather. It didn't look promising—the governor of Missouri had declared a state of emergency, businesses were closing, accidents were being reported. I never let weather stop me from driving somewhere. However, I discussed it with my husband and we decided the right next thing to do would be to cancel the trip. I was so disappointed.

But the silver lining in the ice storm cloud was this: powering through with my plans would show my kids an example of poor judgment that might have ended badly. On the other hand, cancelling showed an example of accepting God's will and not fighting it. Our decision demonstrated flexibility in the light of changing circumstances and priorities. This was life on life's terms.

Panic Attacks   January 17

My first panic attack hit when I was in withdrawal from alcohol and in treatment. I didn't know what it was. In retrospect, it makes sense that a panic attack would show up then; I no longer had my coping mechanism to keep the fear at bay, so I was a raw nerve. The treatment people were no strangers to panic attacks. They identified it for me. The power of panic attacks was that I didn't know what they were. It was pure strong emotion, baffling and scary.

So, the next time the panic started to overwhelm me, in the middle of the night, I said to myself "Oh, so this is what a panic attack feels like." Its power diminished, because I had named it. Then, even better, I joked with it, "So, panic attack, you aren't so bad. Is this all you got?" It went away and I've not had one since, in thirteen years. Panic attacks are powerful. But armed with a little knowledge and self-awareness, I'm more powerful.

Last week, I felt under pressure. I got up at 4 am several times to start work because I had so many commitments in my day I didn't know how else it would get done. I had a strong sense I was getting off on the control, making my productivity my Higher Power. On Sunday, I went to my WA meeting and committed to the following:

(a) I would ask God for help in my morning prayers "help me to not make control and productivity my Higher Power today."

(b) I wouldn't start work before 8:30 am for the next week; and

(c) I would increase my meditation from 10 minutes to 30 minutes each day for the next week.

The first one wasn't so tough, but I didn't want to commit to the second and third. So today I'm done with the week in which I kept these commitments. I have to admit not being able to start work until 8:30 made a huge difference in my attitude. I woke up at 2:30, 3:30, 4:30, 5:30, but each time I told myself I may as well go back to sleep because I wouldn't be able to work for hours.

When I got up at 6:30, instead of feeling pressure, I had a lovely sense of luxuriousness, taking time for coffee with my husband before he left for work, spending quality time with the dogs at the park, getting ready and not looking at my watch during any of it. I meditated for 15 minutes in the morning before 8:30, and then did another 15 minutes around lunchtime. This too was calming. Instead of fewer minutes to be productive, it felt reinvigorating and helped me set my priorities for the rest of the day.

Setting my intention in my morning prayers to be on the lookout for making control and productivity my HP was also helpful. When I felt the urge to start running the show, I could laugh at myself, back off, and ask "How important is it anyway?"

In fact, it worked so well I think I'll commit to it for another week.

Using the Tools   January 19

I felt moved by my Higher Power to teach. I got a gig teaching a class at the law school where I knew many of teachers because I had gotten my Masters in law there. The commitment was three hours of class time a week, for ten weeks. I spent forty hours preparing for classes one and two. It was then I realized I was unprepared for weeks 3-10, and had no time left to prepare those classes to my high standards. My addict told me to quit mid-semester, leaving the school, the students and the teachers high and dry. I was totally screwed and my only option left me utterly humiliated in my profession. My sponsor helped me through it.

First, she helped me get honest that I was new at this. The school and the students didn't expect from me the performance and experience of a 20-year veteran. I *did* have something valuable to offer—real world experience and practical advice, even if I hadn't memorized every case out there.

Then, she helped me get practical with my classes. Did I know any teachers I could ask for advice? Well, yes, two of sisters are teachers. They suggested delegation. So, the next class I went prepared with a list of topics for the students to research and give presentations on over the next six classes. I lined up guest speakers—tapping into my large network of people in this industry—for one hour of each of the remaining classes. With that much content taken off of my hands, I had enough time to pull together lectures for what remained. It was awesome. I got positive feedback from the students on the evaluations, and everyone appreciated the variety of different speakers.

Honesty, acceptance of my imperfections, asking for help, and delegation helped me conquer a predicament instead of running away from it. My disease would prefer I default to self-destruction, but my solution shows me how to make lemonade out of lemons.

Literature   January 20

Reading WA publications on a daily basis impresses the truth upon us and expands our horizons. Such writings can provide information, insight, inspiration and hope. They are available at times when other WA members are not. Further, they provide a comprehensive chronicle of the knowledge of recovery from a multitude of sources. We also study the literature of AA and other Twelve Step programs to strengthen our understanding of compulsive disease. We can identify with many of the situations described by substituting terms like "compulsive working" in place of the named substances and processes.—*The Workaholics Anonymous Book of Recovery*, 2nd Edition.

Every year, I select two daily meditation books to read from each morning in that year. My selections are from different 12-Step programs and other spiritual practices. I see this as part of my 11th step practice—to improve my conscious contact with God. Mornings for me are the height of my workaholism. It is when I'm most convinced I cannot get everything done today. In this way I start my day with new spiritual perspectives that lift me out of my mundane, material fears.

Outlining a Project   January 21

My work addiction, if not treated, forces me to make bad decisions which are not in line with my values, but motivated by fear and ambition. One weekend I learned a valuable lesson about the power of my disease and the power of our solution.

On Friday at work I learned that I had a deadline on Tuesday to submit a written pitch for a huge project for a new client. I had promised my six year old and sister-in-law a weekend away at a waterpark. My disease told me I needed at least ten hours to pull this together, and that would require that I back out of the mini vacation. My disease thinks in black and white, all or nothing. It knows no compromise. The imperious itch must be scratched.

My sponsor had other ideas. She said I needed to go on the getaway weekend. She encouraged me to spend three hours working while the others were sleeping on Saturday morning. This would be enough time to organize my thoughts on paper and create files to hold my writings on each piece of the project. So, I packed a pad of paper and a dozen manila folders and worked on the floor of the bathroom, where I turned on a light in our otherwise dark hotel room. After I got organized, I could breathe. I had a feasible blueprint for what I needed to do on Monday. I spent the time I needed on Monday to pull together the pieces and submitted an excellent proposal on Tuesday. We didn't get the job, but that wasn't the point. I kept my promise to my child while also meeting my professional commitments.

Illness   January 22

On Saturday I planned to attend a large protest march. However, Friday night I started coming down with something—chills, nausea, hurt all over. I wrestled all night with the question of whether I would be well enough in the morning to go to the march.

On Saturday morning, I felt a little better, but not well enough to face what could be many hours on my feet outside at the rally and march. I let my friends know I wouldn't be able to join them. I contacted one of my program friends and committed I wasn't going to do anything that day, except lay low. I needed to take care of my dogs because my family was on a college visit for my youngest. But besides dog care, I planned to watch a few movies and follow the protest developments on Facebook. Although I felt like a truck had run over me physically, my brain functioned enough to passively take information in, around naps.

I didn't beat myself up for missing the rally and for skipping the things I usually do on Saturdays, like pray, write in this book, wash dishes, other chores, 10th step inventory, etc. I kept to my lay-low plan and enjoyed the benefits of relaxation and repair of my broken body. Today (Sunday), I feel one hundred times better and so glad I listened to my body.

Multiple Programs   January 23

I work several 12-Step programs. I'm embarrassed to say how many. That may seem intimidating for an activity addict. How to do it non-addictively? I must be okay with doing each of them imperfectly. I have one life, so I need one recovery program. I take a sponsor from this one and a sponsee from that one, a meeting here and a meeting there. I go to four 12-Step meetings a week. Although the first step in each program is different—I'm powerless over various things—the other 11 steps are identical. I need to tweak my 4th step to include new resentments, fears and harms revealed by my awareness of a new addiction. I don't need to re-do the work I did on the original 4th step. Same with the 6th step—I need to include the new shortcomings that peeling the onion another layer showed me, but I needn't go back and work on the defects detected earlier.

I still do one 10th step inventory a day, and I pray and meditate the same regardless of how many programs I'm in. I meet with one sponsor each week and keep her apprised of my issues regardless of which fellowship is implicated. I keep my other sponsors on my board of advisors for special consultation when needed for a particular addiction. I have five sponsees with whom I'm working the steps.

All in all, it works and it is feasible, and rather than making my life unmanageable, it gives me back my life. I wouldn't trade any of my programs for the world.

Writing   January 24

Journaling is helpful to clarify our thoughts and helps us get to the root of feelings that lie behind our compulsive working. As with reading and meditating, getting our ideas on paper is an option at times with other WA members are not around to listen –with the added benefit that we are able to express ourselves more freely when we need have no regard for the audience. Sometimes just making notes of seemingly important memories or ideas can help quiet the mind as we assure ourselves that they will not be forgotten and can be revisited anytime in the future. Writings can ultimately be shared with others if we so desire.—*The Workaholics Anonymous Book of Recovery*, 2nd Edition.

I use the tool of writing each night when I do my 10th step inventory. I reflect on the events of the day and jot them down. This helps bring to the forefront of my mind the interactions I've had with people or with my addictive thinking. Then I can reflect on situations that might need further attention, such as an amends, or a discussion with my sponsor.

Writing has helped me when I'm anxious and awake in the middle of the night. When I write about my current obsession, instead of going on forever, bouncing around my brain, it now has a beginning and an end. My pain is this big and no bigger. I can write a letter to God. It is a more concrete form of surrender. I can email my sponsor and other program friends about it, without concern I'm waking them up.

Reading Addiction   January 25

At one point, I struggled with reading too much fiction. I read too late into the night, not getting enough sleep. I read page-turners that had me on the edge of my seat instead of making my eyes heavy and ready for sleep. I read in between every chore. The phone rang with a recovery person calling, and I let it go to voicemail. I couldn't wait to get back to my book and I read instead of doing my prayer and meditation in the morning. I wasn't walking the dog as much or hanging with my family as much. At the worst point, I quit doing my chores or put them off until the last minute. I admitted my life was becoming unmanageable and I was powerless over reading fiction.

I checked online for a 12-Step program for reading addiction, but none existed. I decided I had to analogize to other 12-Steps programs. The most helpful tools were to (a) talk to my sponsor and (b) set bottom lines. I committed to my sponsor I wouldn't read past midnight. I agreed if I read a book that is so intense I obsess about getting back to it, skimping on work or self-care, or breaking other bottom lines in other programs, then I have to stop reading it for a week and see what happens. I agreed to set a timer for a predetermined time for reading for the day or in a given sitting.

Once I established the bottom lines, the addiction to reading fiction disappeared. It returned to its rightful, right-sized place in my life, so I enjoyed reading but it didn't eclipse other important parts of my life.

Politics and Media addiction   January 26

Social media reflects articles and videos chronicling a divisive chapter in America's history. There are endless calls to action. I can spend hours reading the stories and signing on-line petitions. My email box is overflowing with requests for donations for worthy causes. I go to bed feeling scared and hopeless.

One can burn out on activism and service as easily as paid work. This is a job for my Higher Power. Not that God will replace my taking appropriate actions to perform my civic duty. But I need to trust God will show me his will and it will be enough that I do it. It's not my job to save the world.

As an addict, my life got small and selfish. I pay no attention to problems in the world and had no energy to invest in it. Now that I'm in recovery, I concern myself more with the future of our planet and democracy. The 2016 presidential election is the first election in which I voted in 30 years. I now sponsor people and help others with their recovery. My Higher Power has told me it is enough for me to keep helping other addicts break out of their addiction. Then they too may find the world gets bigger and they want to contribute. In this small way, I do my part.

If you get tired, learn to rest, not to quit!—Banksy

Spiritual Awakening   January 27

The AA Twelve Steps and Twelve Traditions says "When a man or a woman has a spiritual awakening, the most important meaning of it is that he has now become able to do, feel, and believe that which he could not do before on his unaided strength and resources alone."

My spiritual awakening was of the educational variety and not of the burning bush type. Over time and working the steps, suiting up and showing up, I started to do, feel and believe things which had been impossible for me. When I came into recovery, I just wanted to get rid of my addictions. But I got so much more. Here is a sample, in no particular order of importance:

- I eat healthy every day.
- I don't drive more than 10 miles over the speed limit.
- Perhaps as a result of seeing the miracles in my life, two of my sisters entered recovery.
- I get 7 hours of sleep a night.
- I'm honest about how much time I spend working when I'm at work.
- I get regular medical/dental checkups.
- I believe in God.
- I am committed to being of service to others and it frees me from the bondage of self.
- I have stayed the same weight for 11 years.
- I don't tell my husband what to do.
- I don't gossip.
- I confront people when their behavior calls for it.
- My extended family members ask me for advice and trust me with their secrets.
- I have self-esteem and like what I see in the mirror.
- The light bulbs at my house get replaced when they go out.
- I don't text or email while driving.
- I'll be ok if I lose my job.
- I floss my teeth.
- I get enough exercise but don't abuse my body with it.

- Because I no longer run away from problems at work, I've had amazing success there.
- I intuitively know how to handle many situations which used to baffle me.
- My phone rings all the time with people who love me.

Action Plan   January 28

I took a moment to make an action plan and got immediate relief. It brought the spinning in my head to an end and I wasn't so overwhelmed. My list contained a finite number of tasks and I felt motivated instead of wanting to go back to bed. Amazing.

My gratitude tonight: despite a crushing anxiety today that I wouldn't accomplish everything I wanted, I didn't mistreat anyone and, in fact, managed to pass for reasonably sane.

Amends to Self   January 29

When I came into recovery, the immediate focus was for me to get out of my selfish, self-absorbed focus. My 9th step amends focused on the ways I harmed other people. But, when I began to look at the harm caused by my work addiction, my sponsor had me turn the focus to the harm my disease had caused *me*. Here's the amends letter I wrote to myself:

"I owe you amends for the harm I caused you. Because I didn't know any better, I neglected to take care of you as I should. I didn't let you go to the bathroom when needed. I didn't let you sleep when you were tired. I didn't let you exercise. I didn't feed you good food. I forced you to eat too much food. I starved you. I forced you to exercise more than was healthy for you. I endangered your life by driving too fast to get to work or a work meeting, and by forcing you to multitask while driving. I forced you to be consumed with work so you had to take Sominex every night.

"Because I didn't know any better, I shamed you by telling you you're inadequate. I berated you when you made mistakes instead of using the experience to teach you. I made you believe you should have already mastered everything even when you were doing it for the first time. I compared you unfavorably to other people.I was hard on you by not letting you spend time with friends, by not being patient with you, by not letting you play or relax or take breaks, by making you believe

20

you had to do everything yourself instead of helping you delegate. I forced you to work under pressure and abuse your body with adrenaline. I forced you to race to work and be at work when you didn't need to so you didn't miss some imagined opportunity. I told you that you couldn't trust God or other people to take care of you.

"I forced you to quit jobs in fits of embarrassment rather than work through them and learn. I forced you to spend hours and days nursing resentments. I forced you to be so preoccupied with yourself that you were afraid to try new challenges or speak publicly for fear you wouldn't look good. I forced you to worry endlessly. I told you that you have no value apart from your accomplishments/title/position and I forced you to obsess about other people.

"I regret the harm I caused you and I promise to try not to do these things anymore. I'm so grateful to be a part of your life. You have grown so much in the last six years, and I'm proud of you. You have courage and strength to keep facing the next challenge and not run away. You are smart and you're a good mom, wife, daughter, sister and sponsor."

Being Gentle with Myself   January 30

A note from my journal the first year of my workaholic recovery: "I looked at my schedule for Thursday and Friday and realized it is inefficient for me to go into work for what would amount to a couple hours each day. I let myself off the hook and I'm working from home those two days. A choice in favor of being instead of doing. I feared taking off two days so soon after vacation; what will people think? And I did it anyway."

And you know what I wrote on Thursday and Friday? I acknowledged I'd made the right decision. I was every bit as responsive and productive in my work from home.

Fears   January 31

Often the changes I experience in recovery are so gradual and non-quantifiable I don't even realize I'm making progress. My recent 7th step work revealed that my recovery work removed many of my fears. My sponsor encouraged me to review my previous written fear inventories, and note the ones that don't trouble me today:

- I used to be afraid I'd hurt myself and not be able to run to keep my weight under control; now I can take injury in stride because I'm not binging on food.
- In the past, I was afraid I would get caught stealing, but I got rid of that fear by stopping the behavior.
- I was afraid people would catch on how bad my drinking was because I couldn't remember things in blackouts. I got rid of that fear by stopping the behavior.
- I used to be afraid to be late to anything, but I have a more practical approach now. I evaluate each situation based on how problematic it would be to be late and take appropriate steps.
- I feared returning to work after vacation because my inbox would be overwhelming. I have learned a new behavior in recovery that removes this fear and relaxes me.
- I was afraid I wouldn't be a good sponsor. My experience sponsoring has shown me I'm a good sponsor and all I have to do is try, and the rest is up to the sponsee.
- I used to be afraid when my kids are older, they would not want me in their lives. I'm not concerned with this anymore. Whatever they are available for, I can be grateful and I have plenty of other interests to keep myself occupied and happy.
- I was afraid my kids would die before me and I wouldn't be able to handle it. I don't feel this way presently. I trust God will take care of me. If he takes my kids, that it is his plan. Although it will hurt like a son of a bitch, I will be ok and my experience might even be useful to others.
- I feared getting fat. Today, I trust in my HP and my Overeaters Anonymous program.
- I feared my husband wouldn't love me anymore. I don't worry about this nowadays. If it is God's will, he will love me. If not, I will be ok.
- I was afraid I will spoil my kids. Today, they are far along in their development and don't seem spoiled.
- I used to be afraid of getting caught in traffic jams—mostly because I would be late. Today, I don't worry about this too much; I try to pass the time talking with whoever is with me, or on the phone or meditating.

- I feared sleepless nights—I wouldn't be able to handle what I needed to the next day. I don't worry about this too much presently; I can handle my day even on less than perfect sleep.
- I was afraid of losing my job. Today, since I'm self-employed, I don't worry about people seeing me as a drain on resources and making unilateral decisions that affect my life. If the firm goes under, I can always set up shop on my own or join another firm.
- I used to be afraid my work colleagues would figure out I'm not as good as I'm supposed to be. I don't worry about this lately, although I still struggle with trying to impress people.
- I feared economic insecurity. More recently, I think my husband and I have adequate savings and assets, and good prospects for the future.
- I was afraid to look foolish. I'm not so concerned about this any longer. For instance, I recently got up and poked fun at myself by singing and dancing at my law partner retreat. I'm more likely to say things to clients that are a little off the wall, instead of always being so straight-laced.
- I used to be afraid if I'm not at my desk, I might miss some work opportunity. Today, I trust I can leave my office to take care of errands, etc., and the client will not find another attorney in my absence. If they do, then I don't want to work for that client.
- I feared living with chronic, extreme physical pain. Today, I trust the future will take care of itself and if I'm given pain, I'll also get some really good drugs.

So, as you can see, the burden of all of these fears weighed me down. Recovery has worked its magic to relieve me. Of course, I still have fears, but not nearly as many as before, and faith envelops me to provide a more peaceful existence if I do the spiritual work.

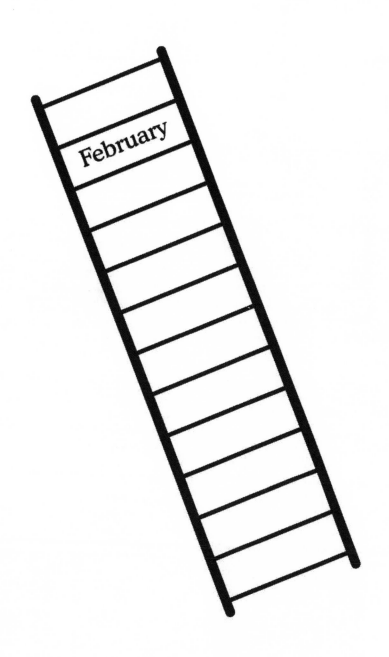

Mistakes   February 1

I used to get upset when I made a mistake at work or someone on my staff made a mistake. I was going to look incompetent in the client's eyes, maybe the client would even fire me. Once I got into recovery, I started asking myself:

- How important is it?
- So what if I look incompetent?
- So what if the client fires me? I'll get others.
- So what if I lose my job? I'll get another one.

I started telling my staff if they weren't making mistakes at least 5% of the time, then they were moving too slowly, checking and double-checking to ensure everything was error-free. Most clients can't afford that kind of service, and most jobs don't call for that level of perfection. We could all breathe easier in this new work culture.

Mistakes are part of the human condition. Recovery has shown me that most errors I make are correctable through the amends process. I now allow myself to lighten up and accept my own and my staff's humanity.

Playing   February 2

We allow ourselves to have fun and play without making it into a work project. – The Workaholics Anonymous Book of Recovery, 2nd Edition, p. 30.

Step 2 holds a promise of a return to sanity. Playing allows me to relax, have fun and enjoy the fruits of my labor and my relationships with other people. It can restore me to sanity by allowing me to laugh and not be so concerned with being productive. It refreshes me and readies me for the next task. It helps my relationships, so there are good times to remember and not just serious ones. Playing could be going for a walk, watching a TV show, riding a roller coaster, playing a game, taking a zipline tour—or whatever silliness doesn't accomplish a single thing on my to-do list.

Public Speaking   February 3

A client asked me to give his staff a two-day legal seminar. I could think of nothing I wanted to do less. I tried to dodge it any way possible. When I concluded there was no escape, I started taking suggestions from my sponsor about how to get through it. I used the tool of delegation and enlisted help from my partners so I didn't have to prepare for and do every presentation.

I prepared my sessions. Because the client couldn't afford for me to spend as much time as I would have liked, I had to content myself with "B"level work. It was hard to not spend the extra time to bring them up to A+. I always considered it a virtue to insist on "A" level work. But now I see it is a character defect. I need God's help with this.

My sponsor encouraged me to follow up with the other speakers a week before the seminar, to ensure their preparation and readiness. What would I do if one of them failed to show? I needed to be ready with at least a "C"level substitute, to avoid getting an "F" altogether for a no-show. I didn't want to contemplate this, but it was a more realistic problem than my disease whispering for me to keep polishing my pieces of the presentation.

The big day came and the presentations went great. Everyone showed up prepared. No technical glitches. The client said "if this wasn't bells and whistles, I don't know what would be." I got to spend a lot of quality time with the clients and they rewarded me by giving my firm a big piece of work.

Stepping Out of my Comfort Zone   February 4

I got a call from a former client. He's on the board of an advertising agency and wanted to know if I'd accept a nomination to join the board. I worked at an ad agency for ten years and helped many ad agency clients for 20 years since then, always in the legal capacity. I've never been on the board of a for-profit organization and had mixed feelings.

On one hand, it seemed like a lot of work and outside of my comfort zone. I'm not a big strategic thinker or a financial whiz. If I do one thing well, it is give legal advice and I wouldn't even be able to do that. In fact, it is a conflict of interest for board members to direct work to their own firms, so I could have no expectation of business from the ad agency. On the other hand, my ego was stoked and I liked the idea of telling people "I can't meet then, I'll be at a board meeting." I was flattered that he even asked me to consider it.

I discussed it with a few program people and my sponsor. My sponsor reminded me being on boards is a nice way to earn extra income in retirement. She encouraged me because it is outside of my comfort zone. Also, there's little risk on my part. If I find I don't like it, I can quit. If they make a mistake in choosing me, they have more to lose. So, I told my former client I was available to interview.

The night before the preliminary phone interview, I researched for an hour the kinds of questions I should expect and what I should be asking. I took some notes. It was a miracle of recovery I didn't type up my notes because I was tempted to, but I realized that would have been perfectionistic. The interview went well.

I heard a week later from my former client they chose another candidate who had significant experience on boards. But he told me every person who had vetted my candidacy had asked "Why isn't this person our lawyer?" My former client said he would introduce me to his CFO who manages their law firms. He said he hoped to bring me in soon for lunch with her and show me around. A week later I had my first assignment from them and they became a client of my firm.

So, here was yet another example of how God keeps giving me more than I want for myself. I had zero expectations of getting legal work from this client, I was willing to try something new, and God rewarded me for just being open.

There is freedom waiting for you, on the breezes of the sky, and you ask "What if I fall?" Oh but my darling, what if you fly?–Erin Hanson

Authority Figures   February 5

I have had an unhealthy relationship with authority figures. I sought my parents' approval and couldn't get enough. I excelled in school and yet the approval of my teachers was never enough. I lacked an internal barometer to encourage me to do the right thing because it was right thing to do. I did the right thing to gain approval from an authority figure, or to avoid disappointing one.

I had major upheavals in school when teachers didn't think I walked on water and I skirmished with the administration about them.

I have since made amends, because I can see now this is part of my disease.

And then there were my bosses. What I wouldn't do to get their affirmation. And then there was a sponsor, once I hit recovery. I completed the steps the first time thanks to people-pleasing my sponsor. Well, sometimes my will and God's will coincide; it was the right next thing to do. I leveraged my character defects to get through those steps.

Today, I need to be careful not to people-please my clients. I try to take a careful look at my motives. Am I saying "yes" because it is in everyone's best interests? Or am I compromising my self-care or boundaries to keep a client happy, because I fear she will go somewhere else if I don't?

I find that if I'm firm regarding my availability with clients, they are indifferent. They don't need the project done on Monday instead of Tuesday. If I assert myself and show respect for my time, they are often more respectful of me as well. I train them how to treat me.

The only authority figure I need to please today is my Higher Power.

Starfish Story   February 6

An old man was walking on the beach early one morning after a big storm. He found the vast beach littered with starfish as far as the eye could see. He noticed a small boy approaching, occasionally bending down to pick up an object and throw it into the sea.

The man called out, "Good morning! May I ask what it is that you are doing?"

The boy replied, "Throwing starfish into the ocean. The tide has washed them up onto the beach and they can't return to the sea by themselves. When the sun gets high, they will die, unless I throw them back into the water."

The old man replied, "But there must be tens of thousands of starfish on this beach. I'm afraid you won't really be able to make much of a difference." The boy bent down, picked up yet another starfish and threw it as far as he could into the ocean. Then he turned, smiled and said, "It made a difference to that one."—adapted from <u>The Star Thrower</u>, by Loren Eiseley.

I will never have a to-do list that is empty. I will always have more to do. I need to accept this, find joy in having stuff to do, and not wish it away. It's okay to not get it all done.

Performance Evaluations   February 7

I've had many performance evaluations over the years. I was not a humble recipient for most of them. Because I'm such a hard worker, and desirous of the positive feedback I could get from bosses, I had exceptional performance appraisals. 98% positive. The problem lie with the two percent "Opportunities for Improvement." That stuck out like a big red X on the evaluation. It blinded me. I argued with the person giving me the evaluation about how they got the two percent wrong.

I've given a lot of performance evaluations over the years. I can't describe what a joy it is to give one to a humble employee who wants to hear the "Opportunities for Improvement" section. Those experiences revealed to me my problem was not only my ego and perfectionism, but I was lazy and afraid. I didn't want to try anything out of my comfort zone. I might not excel at it and then they would find out I'm not "all that."

Those employees eager to improve—they are the ones who get ahead. My path in my disease, on the other hand, was a recipe for stagnation and disappointment. When I got into recovery,I learned I needed to push myself out of my comfort zone. I had to confront those demons my default wiring told me to run away from. As I started to do so, I began reaping professional rewards I wouldn't even have known I was missing if I'd run away from new opportunities and challenges.

Step 3   February 8

The Big Book of Alcoholics Anonymous is an essential piece of my recovery and I consider myself to be a "Big Book thumper." There is one reading that is particularly applicable to this workaholic, and I change the existing language to first person singular, so it is even more personal to me:

The first requirement is that I be convinced that a life run on self-will can hardly be a success. On that basis I am almost always in collision with something or somebody, even though my motives are good. I try to live by self-propulsion. I am like an actor who wants to run the whole show; I am forever trying to arrange the lights, the ballet, the scenery and the rest of the players in my own way.

If my arrangements would only stay put, if only people would do as I wished, the show would be great. Everybody, including me, would be pleased. Life would be wonderful. In trying to make these arrangements I may sometimes be quite virtuous. I may be kind, considerate, patient, generous; even modest and self-sacrificing. On the other hand, I may be mean, egotistical, selfish and dishonest. But, as with most humans, I am more likely to have varied traits.

What usually happens? The show doesn't come off very well. I begin to think life doesn't treat me right. I decide to exert myself more. I become, on the next occasion, still more demanding or gracious, as the case may be. Still the play does not suit me. Admitting I may be somewhat at fault, I am sure that other people are more to blame. I become angry, indignant, self-pitying.

What is my basic trouble? Am I not really a self-seeker even when trying to be kind? Am I not a victim of the delusion that I can wrest satisfaction and happiness out of this world if I only manage well? Is it not evident to all the rest of the players that these are the things I want? And do not my actions make each of them wish to retaliate, snatching all they can get out of the show? Am I not, even in my best moments, a producer of confusion rather than harmony?

There is more, but you get the idea. I need to let go of "my little plans and designs" and be willing to hear what God wants for me. And I'm always surprised and pleased with the results.

Confrontation   February 9

I have a long history of avoiding confrontation. I don't want to make waves. The only examples of confrontation I had growing up were ugly and unskilled. The dynamic I was familiar with went something like this: ignore the irritation, ignore it some more, suffer like a martyr, and then blowup because I can't take it anymore, having given no indication prior to the blow up that anything was wrong. If I gave any indication, I did it passive aggressively: maybe I talked about you behind your back, or mumbled under my breath so you couldn't hear. Or maybe I punished you without your knowledge.

I carried this dynamic into my adult relationships. I expected people to read my mind and to understand that what they were doing was not okay with me—without giving them the courtesy of a heads up.

And after I blow up, I want to sweep the entire matter under the rug, so no constructive problem-solving ever came of it. The irritation would undoubtedly reoccur in the future, so the cycle repeated itself.

Recovery has taught me to be more direct in my dealings with others. I discuss with my sponsor the issue before I talk to the person in question. I may need to inventory the matter first so I get clarity about what is my stuff and what is theirs. I may need to type up a script, so I'm clear in my communication.

I try to pick appropriate times and places to talk with people about how their behavior affects me. I do it out of earshot of others, and when we're not rushed. I try to use "I statements" such as "when you do ____, I feel ____." I adopt a curious attitude, instead of a blaming one, so as not to put the other person on the defensive.

People in relationships won't always agree on everything. Because conflict is inevitable, confrontation is a necessary part of relationships. A strategy of avoiding confrontation can only be successful for so long, because inevitably I explode, my emotions run the show and that is destructive. It is better to have a sober plan that provides a constructive structure for problem-solving towards a long-term resolution. I can't change the other person or control the outcome of the confrontation, but I can give it better odds of success if I'm willing to do the hard work up front.

Seriousness vs. Silliness   February 10

One of my character defects is being too serious. How can I act "as if" I don't? In some of my emails to my husband, I try to be more playful. I joke more with my work partners. I teased the person who gave the lead at my 12-Step meeting tonight. I bought a funny birthday card for one of my sponsees—inappropriate and irreverent. I'm not doing it to be the class clown or to make people love me. I'm trying to observe life from a lighter angle and bring more levity to serious situations.

12-Step Meetings   February 11

We attend W.A. meetings to learn how the fellowship works, to remind ourselves of how far we have come in recovery and to share our experience, strength and hope with other WA members. —Workaholics Anonymous Book of Recovery, Second Edition, p. 27.

For thirteen years, I have attended four 12-Step meetings a week. My kids were six and eleven when I started. I mention that because making time for meetings is hard when you have responsibilities to kids. I heard the thing I put before my sobriety is the second thing I will lose. So, I went to meetings even though it was hard, so I wouldn't lose my kids.

Meetings are the lifeblood of my recovery. I go there to bring my peeps up to date on where I am and hear where they are at. I go there to share the challenges I'm facing and which tools I'm using to get over them. I go there to meet newcomers so my phone is full of numbers to call during the week. Newcomers remind me how bad it was for me, how I'm powerless and how I don't want to ever go back to that place of unmanageability.

Meetings give me a chance to practice the Traditions in a safe environment. I get to see good and bad examples of how to run business meeting.

I have been to meetings in cities I'm visiting and I have attended phone meetings when I can't get to a face-to-face meeting.

Some meetings have strong sobriety and those are good meetings because I can hear the solution. Some meetings are lacking in sobriety and those are good meetings because I can be an example of sobriety and bring hope.

Meditation   February 12

I recently increased my daily meditation from ten minutes to half an hour a day. This is in reaction to what I sensed was an increase in my obsession with productivity. Meditation not only allows me a time to stop the influx of information from the world around me such as email and social media. It encourages me to turn off the flow of constant chatter in my head for a while. Though I struggle to give my meditation priority and am resistant, when I'm doing it, I feel better for having stopped the flow of information if only for a bit. (I have to admit that I used some of my "meditation" today to compose this entry in my head.)

Maybe when my kids move out, I can meditate. –comment from a young mom at a 12-Step meeting

Face-to-Face Interactions   February 13

In this world of impersonal email, text messages, websites, social media and voicemail, meeting with people face-to-face is powerful.

Many of my clients know me only through email and telephone; we have never met in person. However, if I get the chance, I jump on it. The impact of a brief in-person encounter is evident sometimes for years. They are more loyal to me and I to them. Personal meetings offer more substance and credibility.

I attend four face-to-face 12-Step meetings each week. While I will occasionally phone it in, I prefer to go to in-person meetings, if only to stop myself from multitasking for the duration of the meeting.

For most of my 13 years in recovery, I met with my sponsor in person once a week to work the steps. I encourage my sponsees to meet with me in person instead of over the phone. I prefer it and get more out of it, but often this isn't possible due to time constraints or because the sponsee is in a distant city.

Recovery is a personal, emotional journey. It gets messy. Being face-to-face encourages honesty and intimacy, both of which are difficult for me. My chances of success are better if I'm connecting with people at a gut level, and not sanitized over impersonal media.

Right-sizing Attitude towards Work   February 14

Williams Wordsworth wrote *"The world is too much with us; late and soon, Getting and spending, we lay waste our powers."* That was how I acted towards my work. Fear, perfectionism and obsession bogged me down. I cared little for my opinion of my performance and lived for kudos from others. I talked work to anyone available. I had trouble sleeping, worrying about the future. The weight of my work crushed me.

Recovery showed me that work is like climbing a mountain. It is not easy. There should be challenges, if I'm doing it right. When I reach the goal, I should be satisfied. I can look down and say "I did that" and feel good about myself.

These mountains that you are carrying, you were only supposed to climb. –Najwa Zebian

Gratitude   February 15

Gratitude has played a big role in my recovery journey. In treatment, the counselors told me to make gratitude lists, to focus on what I did have, rather than what I didn't. They said a grateful heart is much closer to my Higher Power than a cynical one.

"What's in it for me?" characterized my life before recovery. I used people and work situations to make myself feel better. Focusing on gratitude represented a paradigm shift.

Today, I do a 10th step inventory each night. The last part of my inventory I write five or so things I'm grateful for. What a pleasant thought on which to slip off to sleep, rather than worrying about the next day. Let's go half full.

Less is Less   February 16

I used to think the more I accomplished in my day, the fewer items there would be on my to-do list. I now question the irrefutable logic of that.

Some items on my to-do list actually increase the total busyness of my life. For instance, doing more marketing will increase my clients roster and therefore the number of assignments. Spending time on media will increase the number of articles I feel compelled to read. In a commencement address at Yale, Tom Hanks noted that "boredom is vanquished" because there is always something to do online.

Therefore, it is incumbent on me to take myself out of the stream more, rather than less. Meditate, listen to music, exercise, play games. Slow down. The less I do, the less I'll have to do.

Humility   February 17

I struggle with humility. I understand I need it to stay sober. But after years in recovery, it is hard not to be complacent, to think I've got addiction figured out. Hell, I'm writing a book on recovery. That isn't humble.

And thinking "I've got this" is my disease. I need to stay in touch with how powerless I am over my addictions. I need constant reminders. When I go to a meeting, hear the literature and identify yet again, that creates humility. When I speak to a newcomer, hear their struggles and am reminded of my past, that creates humility.

Working the steps created humility in me. First, coming out of my denial and admitting I was powerless was huge. Conceding maybe I was wrong about the existence of a Higher Power, that was humbling. Turning over control to my Higher Power moment-by-moment every day, that is necessary to right-size me.

One of my prayers at night (on my knees, out loud, which helps me stay humble) is "Show me how to be your servant." This language is poignant and repugnant to my disease.

The 4th step inventory changed my righteousness and got me to see how I'm the problem. Admitting my character defects (as yet undisclosed to anyone) to my sponsor in my 5th step were the single most humbling moments in my life. The 6th and 7th steps, with their focus on my shortcomings, made obvious I was not yet perfect and the job continues.

Making amends in 8 and 9 was a solid dose of humility with each one. Writing an inventory in Step 10 continues to reveal to me when and where I mess up. Step 11 encourages me to keep seeking my Higher Power's guidance instead of relying on my imperfect self.

And finally, Step 12, with its talk of practicing these principles in all my affairs, has forced me to peel the onion to reveal further layers needing work, a humbling state which has convinced me I will never be done, and that is okay.

Hearing a 5th Step   February 18

The disease of workaholism is a lonely place. Whether I'm working late or immersed in checking tasks off my to-do list, I'm getting a rush from productivity. I'm not being intimate with anyone. Workaholism is the opposite of emotional intimacy.

Hearing someone's 5th step, on the other hand, is the epitome of intimacy. As a sponsor in WA, I'm honored when a sponsee asks me to hear her fifth step. For her to trust me with her secrets and witness the baring of her soul is a profound act of closeness which I'm not sure exists outside 12-Step recovery. I try to share how I've said and done similarly unattractive things, because it is our weakness that binds us, not our strength. It brings me closer to another human being about something that matters spiritually. It acts as an antidote for my workaholism.

Intimacy = into me you see.—overheard at a WA meeting.

Decisiveness   February 19

I consider myself to be a decisive person. This comes from the enormous discomfort I feel when I don't know what's next. I have a low tolerance for ambiguity. When I'm in the process of making a decision, I obsess. I worry it like a dog with a bone. Whether the decision is a big one or a small one doesn't seem to matter: the fact it is *undecided* is the problem. "Should I take this job?" or "what's for dinner?" Both receive similar energy. It's nuts. And as soon as I make a decision, the obsession and discomfort disappear. Thus, quite of bit of shooting from the hip.

I believe God doesn't care what decisions I make about most situations and there is not one right way to wind myself through this life. God has given me a big hoop, with wide margins, and the hoop is not on fire. Of course, life goes better for me when I do the next right thing and avoid lying, cheating and stealing. However, whether I take this job or that, or whether I marry this person or that, my challenge is to find a way to live well regardless of the choices I make.

Image Management   February 20

One of my character defects is excessive concern about how I appear to other people. This goes hand in hand with people pleasing, even at the expense of my own needs. I went through life asking myself "What does he think of me?" and "What does she think of me?" I asked it if the person in question was my boss or the cashier at the grocery store. Sadly, I can never know the true answer. Even if I ask the person, they may not tell me the truth, and it's not my business.

Recovery taught me that the correct questions to be asking are "What do I think of me?" and "What does God think of me?" If I am satisfied with the answers to *those* questions, then all will work out and I can be at peace in the meantime.

An affirmation I can use here: "I have God's approval, attention and love."

HALT   February 21

When I got into recovery, I learned I should avoid "HALT" which stands for Hungry, Angry, Lonely and Tired. When I'm in HALT, I make bad decisions.

These situations are stressors for me. If I'm in HALT, it means I'm not using good self-care. I need to take the corrective actions necessary to get out of HALT, and then turn back to making decisions and taking actions. For hunger, I need to eat nutritious food. For anger, I need to do a resentment inventory. For loneliness, I need to call someone or schedule social time. Sometimes, going to bed is hard for me. I have "experience greed" and don't want to miss anything. But, if I'm tired, "even when offered the best, say no if I need the rest."

Trust   February 22

When I came into the rooms of 12-Step recovery, I was ready to trust. I was out of any better ideas. I couldn't believe it had come to this, but what choice did I have? I jumped in with both feet. I trusted my sponsor. I trusted the people who spoke at meetings. I trusted these people had struggled with the problems I was experiencing—how could I not? They were telling my story. And I trusted if I did what they did, I would someday receive the gifts they seem to be enjoying in their lives: serenity, integrity, good relationships, balance, financial security and love. And eventually, I trusted in a God of my understanding.

Shame   February 23

Here's an example of how shame can come up for me: a new law comes out in my field. Nobody understands it, because the law is new. Every lawyer will need to research, analyze and analogize how the change will affect their clients. Other lawyers will not know how the regulators will interpret and enforce the law. A client calls and wants advice on the new law. My addict tells me to charge the client for one hour, even though I will spend ten hours doing the research necessary to give them the advice. I'm ashamed I'm not an expert already, and the client shouldn't pay for my shortcomings. This is insane. The client would have to pay any other attorney to research the new law.

I understand now this is my ego. My ego says I should be better than others. Other people get the opportunity to learn new things. But for me, the bar is higher. I don't get to be a newcomer, to not know how to do new stuff. Thankfully, with this awareness, I can get relief from my shame.

Logic   February 24

I used to thrive on my logic. Creativity, intuition and spirituality had no place in my life. That touchy-feely stuff made me ill. I prided myself on not believing in God. God was a mechanism those in power used to keep the masses in check. It was for the weak and ignorant. God was so illogical.

Recovery has been a humbling experience for my ego. I had to concede logic does not trump intuition. Logic dictated I need to look out for myself, when in reality, I am taken care of fine when my focus is on others. My best moments in recovery are when I set aside logic and try to channel my Higher Power. It helps me find the right words in a difficult conversation or pick a direction at a fork in the road.

Resentments   February 25

Before I got into recovery, I didn't understand resentment. I learned when a person hurts me, it's normal for me to feel hurt. But a resentment literally means to "re-feel." And I played that sucker over and over in my head, re-hurting myself.

I got into recovery when I was forty, and I did my 4th step that year. In my forty years, I had accumulated seventy-one resentments, which amounted to forty-six typed pages. Doing the four-column resentment inventory from the AA Big Book changed my life.

I've been in recovery thirteen years, and I have written another seventy-five pages of resentment inventories because I keep it current. I hate the way resentment makes me feel. I don't want to live with it one minute longer than I have to. I was a victim all the time. Nothing was ever my fault. The resentment inventory showed me if the other guy is the problem, I'm fucked. But if I'm the problem, I can do something about it. And that is freedom.

In my experience, three possible next steps come out of an inventory: (a) I need to make an amends; (b) I realize I'm the problem and I don't need to do anything; or (c) I need to confront someone else with their bad behavior, or as my sponsor likes to say, with how their behavior makes me feel.

The good news is, the resentment disappears and I can either try to fix the situation or let it go.

Obsession   February 26

When I am in my addiction, I can spend hours scheming and fantasizing over a work dilemma. What can I research to optimize my success? Who should I rally to my side? I can toss and turn at night drafting the perfect email in my head to make myself look good. Who should I copy? My ambition knows no bounds.

If I'm having a good day, I talk with my sponsor. Being honest challenges me. I'm only as sick as my secrets, and what I feed grows, but what I starve dies. When I deprive my addiction of what it needs (dwelling on unhealthy trains of thought, dishonesty), little by little workaholism loses its power over me.

Being Flexible   February 27

One of my paralegals, Michael, was driving me crazy. I emailed him assignments, and he didn't respond. I followed up via email a week later, and still no response. Michael is an excellent paralegal, super smart, but I was at the end of my rope with his lack of responsiveness and ready to fire him. I carried a massive resentment and felt like such a victim.

I talked to my sponsor. She asked if I knew other people at the firm Michael worked well with, and how that looked. I said I noticed him sitting in the office of another attorney regularly. My sponsor suggested I try meeting with Michael to discuss the open items and see what happens. I hated this suggestion because I didn't want another meeting on my calendar. Besides, he was the paralegal, he should adjust to my requirements. Nevertheless, I took her suggestion.

I put a meeting on the calendar for every Tuesday at 10 am. Lo and behold, every Friday I got a steady stream of emails from Michael on the open items. He showed up in my office on Tuesdays with everything either done or in someone else's court.

We worked well together for many years thereafter. We met every week. He did my assignments in a timely manner. He didn't want to face me in person and say he hadn't moved the ball forward. I was ecstatic. My work was getting done, I didn't need to fire an excellent paralegal. I no longer cared I had an extra meeting on my calendar—it was always a short one.

I am lazy and not interested in doing the hard work of changing. I am selfish and prefer the other guy do the hard work of changing. But, if it's in my power to fix the situation by changing, who is really the problem?

God loves me so much right where I am, but also too much to let me stay there. –overheard at a WA meeting

Procrastination   February 28

Even though I'm a workaholic, procrastination is one of my defects of character. I chomp at the bit to do the sexy jobs. The unglamorous ones can back up on me, especially if they don't have any deadline. I start to lose sleep, wondering when my procrastination is going to get so out of control my life is unmanageable.

When I was working on my 6th step, my sponsor suggested I talk to God about it, and here's what he said: "Grownups take responsibility. There's enough drama in life you don't need to add to it by creating pressure by not attending to your responsibilities in a reasonable time." That doesn't mean I have to do them all *now*. It's just I need to adopt an attitude which is not "all or nothing."

Here's an affirmation I can use to help motivate me to do the unsexy stuff: "I can set priorities and attend to tasks in a reasonable time frame."

Urgency   February 29

My disease likes to tell me that everything is urgent. I called my sponsor and left urgent messages. My sponsor said, "Nothing is urgent." As a newbie, that was hard to believe.

I race walked back to the office after a Workaholics Anonymous meeting, because I was afraid if I missed a call from a client, they would go somewhere else. Clients and partners like my sense of urgency. I am known for my responsiveness. I was available on email, even if I was at my kids' games or the grocery store, or on vacation. I'm a lawyer, but the kind of law I practice isn't going to save anyone from the death penalty at the ninth hour. Mostly, it can wait. My sense of urgency is driven by a need to look good, feel important and/or not want the task hanging over my head. I want to impress my partners and clients with how on top of things I am.

So, more and more, I've been taking a "chill pill." When I'm anxious about getting to a particular task, I try to unpack my motivation. Oh, that's just me being self-centered. Urgency isn't warranted. I can do it tomorrow. I have done enough today.

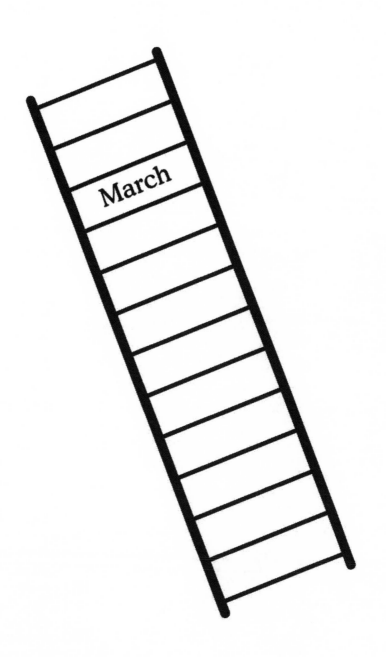

Work Ethic

Good, better, best,
Never let it rest,
'Til your good is better,
And your better is best. – St. Jerome

I remember this rhyme from 3rd grade. This is typical of the messages I heard about how to run my life. Another: "The early bird catches the worm" and "The good is the enemy of the best."

I live in a culture that adores striving for the American Dream. My first jobs in grade school were a paper route, selling seeds and greeting cards door-to-door, babysitting, and shining shoes at a barber shop. I worked through high school as a waitress and as office help at a magazine. I graduated high school in three years by going to summer school, and in my gap year, I worked three part-time jobs.

I went to undergrad and then law school at night, working full-time during the days as a secretary and a paralegal. Later, I got a Masters in law, also at night, while working as a partner at a law firm, with two small children at home.

I was proud of my work ethic. I didn't know there was any other way to be.

Concentrating and Step 2

Step 2 says "Came to believe that a power greater than ourselves could restore us to sanity." When I multitask, I'm acting insanely. When I focus on what I'm doing, part of my brain can connect to my Higher Power. I accomplish the single activity in a way that reflects God's will, which is always sanity.

Choice of Media

Nothing pays off like restraint of tongue and pen. –Twelve Steps and Twelve Traditions of Alcoholics Anonymous, p. 91

And in my case, email, text messages and IM. I used to think nothing of sending emails off to work colleagues, staff, vendors, or my husband regardless of topic. Often, my agenda was to respond quickly so I could check it off my to-do list. Sometimes I would justify it to myself because the other person was in an inconvenient time zone and I'd have to wait until the next day to speak by phone. I didn't care if it was a delicate subject that should be handled in person. I didn't understand how poor a medium email is for communicating nuances. I once emailed my secretary pointing out her "areas for improvement." It didn't go over well.

Today, I try not to send emails or text messages with negative or highly-charged subjects. If possible, I have the conversation in person, with telephone as the next best alternative. If I receive an angry written message from someone else, I pick up the phone. It is amazing what people will type into their phones but won't say directly. Often, when I pick up the phone to discuss an angry message I've received, the sender is like a different person who won't even bring up the subject they just ranted at me about. I like the outcome much better than when I would escalate the situation by responding via email.

Taking Risks   March 4

Two related shortcomings prevent me from trying new things, taking risks and making mistakes: a fear of looking foolish and an inability to take criticism. When my default wiring is calling the shots, I hear, "You're not smart enough" and, regarding negative feedback, "They don't know what they are talking about."

When my Higher Power is calling the shots, I hear, "Welcome feedback from others. Don't shut it out. Other people might know what they are talking about. If you're not making mistakes, you are not using the gifts I gave you to grow. Embrace your humanness. Have a beginner's mind. Develop a sense of humor around it. I don't make junk—I gave you special talents and you are not doing my will when you hide them under a bushel basket."

An affirmation I use to combat these character defects is "It is okay to make mistakes. It is okay to look silly. I have more to offer than I give myself credit for."

Physical Aspects of Workaholism   March 5

I believe workaholism is a disease, that it is both a physical addiction to adrenaline and stress hormones and a process addiction to compulsive activity. There were physical consequences to my addiction. When I was at my worst, I didn't work out—just couldn't make time because I had too many work/household tasks to accomplish.

I paid for a membership at a gym, but never went. Not getting the exercise I need deprives my body of a healthy outlet for my stress, as well as relaxation. In my disease, I have a hard time justifying working out—I can't see immediate results.

For many years, I was "addicted" to Sominex. I would get up at 5 am, work like crazy until 5pm when I picked up the kids, binge on food and drink wine from the moment I walked in the door and started to come off the adrenalin and pass out around 9:30 pm. If I didn't take Sominex, I would wake up at 2 am, start worrying about work and be unable to return to sleep.

When I was forty-three, I developed Hodgkins Lymphoma. I had to take two and one-half months off work. I can't produce evidence that my addiction caused the cancer, but it makes sense my poor health habits—the result of my addiction—compromised my immune system. Lastly, I neglected to floss my teeth, and had several gum recession surgeries as a result.

Today, I strive for thirty minutes of aerobic walking a day, and I achieve it most days. I take spin classes at the YMCA. I eat healthy foods every day and I don't drink alcohol. I don't need Sominex to stay asleep. I tune into my body and rest when I'm tired or sick, noticing when my eyes are tired from too much screen time. And I floss my teeth.

Intensity   March 6

Intensity used to define my way of being in the world. I loved the adrenaline rush I got from making mountains out of molehills. I could fantasize my work and purpose in life to be more glamorous than it was in reality. I sought ways to dramatize my interactions with people at work—casting myself as the hero and them as villains.

Today, I can be okay with a day without drama. Some days are for chopping wood and carrying water and those can be the best days now, instead of days to dread because they are boring. I can smell the flowers and be grateful for little things, such as a walk with my dogs, a TV show with my husband or good news from a sponsee. Today, I trade in the intensity for serenity, and feel I've gotten the better end of the deal.

Wear the world as a loose garment, which touches us in a few places and there lightly. – St. Francis of Assisi.

Success List   March 7

Not long after I began working the first step in Workaholics Anonymous, my sponsor and I were discussing self-esteem. It seems I needed to work on mine. My sponsor suggested I make a list of everything I deemed to be a success in my life. The good news and bad news is the list was too long to include here. I included items from my academic and professional life, relationships with immediate family, extended family, and other relationships, recovery, and self-care.

Reviewing my success list from time to time, and adding to it, is a great reminder how far I have come.

The way to increase self-esteem is to do esteemable acts.

Forgiveness of Others   March 8

I had a very difficult relationship with one of my bosses before I got into recovery. She was a micromanager and hyper-critical of my every move. I had lots of resentments of her which I carried with me for years.

When I got into recovery and learned how to inventory my resentments, I got relief. I also became clear that I owed her amends for my bad behavior in the relationship. This was hard for me because I still considered her behavior as much worse than mine, and that was true. Still, I needed to clean up my side of the street. I realized I couldn't successfully make amends to her until I had forgiven her. So, I worked on that, and began including this in my morning prayers, "God, please grant me the humility to make amends to Jane." After six months of this daily prayer, I felt a softening in my heart about her, and a readiness to set up the amends. It came off without a hitch and we are on friendly terms today. She's not my best friend, but I don't need to cross to the other side of the street when I see her coming.

Surrender   March 9

Step 3 seemed abstract when I first heard it: "Made a decision to turn our will and our lives over to the care of God as we understood God." But I see now it is a daily if not hourly surrender that is practical. For example:

I went to a retreat for a long weekend and when evening came, my phone wouldn't charge. I tried every outlet in the room (which meant moving furniture) and even those in the communal bathroom. Clearly, the cord was no longer functioning. I panicked. My phone represents so much more than a phone. It was my alarm clock, my book, my entertainment, my lifeline to the outside world.

When I had tried all the outlets a second time and jiggled the cord every which way, the idea of surrender entered my head. "God, thank you for this problem. What are you trying to teach me?" Surrender is hard for me when it involves my phone. However, I immediately felt a sense of relief this problem wasn't mine to bear alone and maybe my urgency signaled a larger failure to trust my HP. I went to sleep.

In the morning, I remembered I had a phone charger in my car. I swapped out the cord. Surrendering saved me from a sleepless night. The break I took from trying to muscle my way into a solution allowed intuition and creative thinking in. I could see options other than getting my broken cord to work. And I was saved from a phone-less retreat.

Prayerful Decision-Making   March 10

Sometimes it is hard to know what the next right thing is. Perhaps a number of reasonable choices exist. I can run the scenario past several program people and my sponsor, and still not be sure. I can meditate on it and not be closer to the answer.

One suggestion I've heard is prayerful decision making. It involves imagining myself having chosen a particular option. How would I feel? Tell another person, "This is what I have decided." Does that leave me discordant, or peaceful? Next, try imagining myself having made a different decision. Ask myself the same questions. If fears dissolve, obstacles overcome and details begin falling into place, I'm on the right track.

I had one sponsee who, trying to decide whether to get married, started acting as if she had accepted her boyfriend's proposal. She asked God to send a big sign if she was not doing His will. Having seen no such sign, I got to attend her amazing wedding and today she is the mother of two beautiful kids.

Rewards

While working on Step One with my sponsor, she asked what I would do if I weren't working so much. I hadn't given it much thought, so she suggested that I make a list of ways I might reward myself for having reached a work goal.

Here's my list:

(1) trip to conservatory or Botanic gardens,

(2) massage,

(3) pedicure,

(4) listen to music,

(5) read fiction,

(6) walk the dog,

(7) sit at coffee shop and drink my latte, instead of leaving with it,

(8) read my fiction book on the train home, without using my phone,

(9) having clothes and accessories that fit and match (but I don't like having to shop for them),

(10) eating (abstinently) at restaurants,

(11) taking a nap,

(12) sleeping in,

(13) looking at videos on Youtube,

(14) working out/running,

(15) watching movies/going to movies,

(16) laying on the beach,

(17) enjoying a fire in the fireplace and

(18) going to a 12-Step retreat.

After I read my sponsor the list, she suggested I start doing them. I've gotten better at giving rewards to myself. It was a helpful exercise to identify those activities I find enjoyable and not "productive."

Justification

I think workaholism is an under-diagnosed disease, in part because addicts like me can justify our behavior. Unlike drugs or alcohol, we don't appear to be ruining our lives. Indeed, we appear successful. Here are ways I have rationalized my workaholic behavior:

> Not allowing time for fun in my day because I have too much work to do. My work is more important than having fun and joking around.
> Dropping off my kids at day care when it opened at 7 am and picking them up when it closed at 6 pm, because I wanted to get ahead in my career and the only way was to work every available hour.
> Compulsively checking for new messages when I'm bored. I can tell myself it's vital I'm responsive to my clients and partners.
> Being obsessed with and talking about work incessantly. I didn't know this was wrong or any other way to act. I had many reasons to bitch about work—what every awful person at work had done to me or their incompetence.
> Being jealous of work colleagues. Again, I didn't understand this was wrong. I justified my jealousy by feeding the story in my head: how my colleagues left me out, making it impossible for me to compete and get clients, how I was just born inadequate—not as smart, charismatic, connected.
> Communicating negative information or criticism via emails instead of picking up the phone or doing it in person. I rationalized this indirect behavior by telling myself it was after hours and I needed to respond immediately. Because the subject of my email had left for the day, email was my only option. I also justified it because I needed to cover off several people on the email and I couldn't do that by phone or in person.

Wants vs Needs   March 13

What do I do when my self-care needs conflict with the needs of others in my life? I ran into this when I was in chemotherapy. I got extremely tired at 4pm every day, and needed a nap. My husband wanted to register our youngest for a volleyball camp from 3-5pm on Tuesdays. I told him I was fine with that, provided he drove them. Wouldn't you know it, the first Tuesday of the camp, he had a work conflict and asked me to cover it. I was furious. I called my sponsor. She said, "If your seats recline in your car, can't you nap there?" I couldn't believe it. "You mean I can't even play the cancer card here?"

She said, "It's ok to take care of yourself, but you may need to be creative about how to get your needs met. It may not look exactly the way you want. As long as your needs (not wants) are met, everything you have left over is for service to others." So, I napped in my car.

Third Step Prayer   March 14

Sometimes when I'm in 12-Step meetings, and I hear the pain around me, I'm inclined not to share because my life is actually going well. It seems insensitive to share how good I've got it because it rubs other people's noses in it.

The AA Big Book Third Step prayer says: *God, I offer myself to you to build with me & to do with me as you will. Relieve me of the bondage of self, that I may better do your will. Take away my difficulties, that victory over them may bear witness to those I would help of your power, your love & your way of life.*

I say this prayer every morning. I like that God takes away my difficulties so victory over them bears *witness* to others. Thus, the prayer not only gives me permission to share my successes but mandates it. I'm not hurting fellow sufferers by describing how well the program works: I'm showing them the way. I'm offering hope. If people hadn't done the same for me when I first came in, why would I stay?

Time-Stuffing   March 15

Time-stuffing is spontaneously adding to agendas and cramming another action into every spare minute. I am guilty of this. It is part of my FOMO (Fear of Missing Out). I don't want to miss out on anything. I don't want to let anyone down. Whenever I found myself with a spare minute, I looked for ways to fill it. If someone suggested an activity or outing, I didn't consider my energy level given other commitments that day, but only whether I could logistically pull it off.

Before I got into recovery for workaholism, I didn't realize this was a problem, and I certainly didn't know it had a name.

I remember one small example of time stuffing. I wanted to go to a recovery potluck—it was important to me. But if I went, I needed time to grocery shop, make food and drive 45 minutes to the event, in addition to the 1½ hours at the event. This was on top of an already busy work day. When I stopped and asked my Higher Power for direction, God gave me leave to cut myself some slack, and give up the potluck. I felt such relief. I went about the rest of my day serenely, instead of with urgency.

Today, when I am trying to decide whether to say yes to an activity that will potentially be too much, I try to err on the side of too little. There will always be activities I miss—I can't possible do them all. It's okay if I miss some experiences. My serenity is worth the tradeoff.

Denial   March 16

Before I came into recovery for work addiction, I had no idea I was a work addict. I could see the individual pieces that make up my workaholism but they were meaningless bits of information not yet woven together. I knew:
- I felt urgency at work.
- I multitasked.
- I talked shop nonstop.
- I was scared at my job.
- I felt inadequate as to my work performance.
- I worked when I planned to do something else.
- I read and responded to work emails while driving.
- I worried about work incessantly.

I had no consciousness these represented symptoms of a bigger diagnosis. I was in denial. Diagnosis of workaholism has a long fuse. The circumstances must be just right for someone to break through the denial and see the disease for what it is. Awareness can take many years and false starts. I believe it is God's grace that allowed precisely enough discomfort and self-awareness to coalesce at the same time to get me into the rooms of Workaholics Anonymous. And even now, I frequently forget I'm a work addict and that is just how powerful the denial can be.

Prioritization   March 17

One of the tools of WA recovery is prioritization. I didn't understand prioritization when I first came into WA, but now it is one of my most important tools. Here's an example:

I get many work emails. Before recovery, when returning from vacation, I was a crazy person, trying to address every email, regardless of whether it needed immediate attention. I wouldn't talk to anyone at my office because of my urgency with clearing out my inbox. After being in recovery for a while, it occurred to me to try the tool of prioritization on my emails. I set up special sub-folders in my email: one labelled "Print for filing," one labelled "Needs attention" and one labeled "Urgent." While on vacation, I monitored my emails 15 minutes total a day, and filed them into the folders designating their priority. A select few went into the "Urgent" folder—maybe two hours' worth of work. My first day back in the office, I dealt only with the "Urgent" emails. When I return from vacation is random. It could have been three days, or a week or two weeks. The emails don't know my return date. They can wait a day.

I have now returned from many vacations and had the most serene re-entries. I can take the time to chat with my colleagues about my vacation and ask them how they are. I realize now how self-imposed the pressure was that first day back in the office when I thought I had to do everything right away. My addict likes the adrenalin and feels important when there's urgency.

Compulsively Checking Email   March 18

How many 12-Step programs do I have to work? What if I were addicted to something there wasn't a program for, such as compulsively checking my messages? I'd have to come up with bottom line behaviors on my own. Here's an example: I will not check my messages when I feel a lull in the action, and simply want stimulus. At those times, I'm going to turn to God instead and ask his will. I can check my messages when that bored feeling passes.

Addiction Treatment Programs   March 19

In my experience, treatment served a specific purpose. It educated me about addiction, interrupted my compulsive habits, got me used to discussing difficult subjects with strangers and got me into 12-Step recovery.

I heard this story: A man went to treatment on a luxury liner. When his 30 days were up, the liner threw him into the ocean. A 12-Step rowboat came by and offered to pick him up. He said "No, I'm good." He tread water for a few weeks and the rowboat returned to see if he wanted help. He got in.

I've seen people in 12-Step recovery find it isn't working for them (because they aren't working the steps) and they go into treatment. They are successful in treatment, removed from the challenges of life on life's terms. But then treatment ends and they go back to acting out as before. Of course, everyone's experience is different, but I have never seen treatment work where 12-Step recovery failed. We addicts need to identify ways to be ok in the real world, because treatment inevitably ends. And, from my experience, that means working the 12 Steps.

Workload   March 20

We work at a comfortable pace and rest before we get tired. – The Workaholics Anonymous Book of Recovery, *2nd Edition, p. 30.*

This idea mystified me. Who works at a comfortable pace? I always had adrenalin pumping through me. I always felt pressure to do more and do it faster. Rest was for when the work was done, not something I allowed myself based on how I felt.

In recovery, I learned the amount of work on my desk or on my personal to-do list at any given time is random. Sometimes there's a lot, sometimes not. It is not my job to be sure that everything gets done if it's more than I can soberly do. My job is to:
-   consider available resources for delegation;
-   figure out what can be put off;
-   meditate for inspiration about a way to work smarter instead of harder; and/or
-   communicate to the people depending on me "I can't do it all;" give them an opportunity to revise the deadlines or find another resource to help.

Step Two   March 21

Step Two says "Came to believe that a Power greater than ourselves could restore us to sanity."

When I came into recovery in 2005, I was vehemently agnostic. Although I was raised Catholic, I turned my back on Catholicism in college. I adored logic and God was not logical. I appeared to have success in life by being the master of my own destiny: I had the two-car garage, picket fence, successful career, two kids, and husband. When my aunt gave us a house-warming gift of a plaque which said "God Bless This Home," I refused to accept it.

But hitting bottom with my addictions forced me into 12-Step recovery. In the rooms, I heard countless stories from people who hadn't believed in God, but when they opened themselves to the possibility of a Higher Power, they found faith. They said a HP helped them to recover from their addictions. If it worked for them, maybe it will work for me.

In treatment, they told me I should act "as if" I had a Higher Power and by the 9th month, I might start believing it. My sponsor told me to get on my knees twice a day and pray out loud to a God I didn't believe in. In the mornings, I said prayers from the AA Big Book, and in the evenings I thanked God for letting me be addiction-free today, and for the blessings of that day.

I began asking God for help with my problems. I also told my sponsor and talked about my problems at meetings. I took suggestions and my life started getting better. I think my brain couldn't handle the inconsistency of praying to a God I didn't believe in, and to correct the disconnect, my brain decided God did exist, to rationalize all this praying.

About the 9th month into recovery, I began to sense a presence listening when I prayed. As it turns out, I came to believe in a Power greater than myself, and it restored me to sanity.

Triggers   March 22

I had an unusual experience ordering a diploma frame online for my son's college graduation. We received an ad from a vendor of the prestigious university he attended. I trusted the school implicitly. When I placed my order online, the company tried to scam me by charging me $20 for shipping, when it had lured me in with a $5 shipping promotion. When I online-chatted with a rep from the company, he assured me if I placed the order, he would process a refund for the difference, so I did.

Then he gave me a hard time about refunding the full $15. I was so angry, not only for myself, but for other parents. They might not have 45 minutes to online chat, so they might let it go, allowing the frame company to benefit from their scam.

I never lost my cool with the rep and I treated him respectfully. However, I sent letters of complaint to the University and to the Consumer Protection divisions of the relevant states' Attorneys General, which took hours.

That evening, I was depressed and emotionally hungover. I skipped my usual workout class, and I thought to myself—what can I do that won't be self-destructive? I took a long hot bath because I'd heard people in the rooms of recovery offer baths as a self-care stopgap.

The next day, my sponsor suggested filing online reviews on the company's Facebook page, Yelp, BBB and Ripoff Report,which I did. I know anger has its place, and I was channeling it as constructively as possible.

My sponsor also suggested my reaction might concern something older and deeper. I reflected for next few days. I journaled in my nightly inventory. There was a time when I was young where a person in authority betrayed my trust and hurt me immensely. The situation was different in the details, but my current outrage was about the betrayal, rather than the money. Once I understood I was being triggered, my anger dissipated. This vendor and the University hadn't hurt me that drastically, but because it triggered a strong old emotion in me, I reacted as though they had hurt me as much as the person in my past. I stopped obsessing about the vendor, knowing I had taken reasonable steps to address the scam.

If I'm hysterical, it's historical. – 12-Step saying

Love   March 23

One of the concepts I've heard in recovery is love is an action, not a feeling. All my life, I would have said love is a feeling. It is the rush of pheromones when dating, or the strong attachment to my husband after many years together, the sure knowledge I'd do anything for my kids including take a bullet, or my affection for my dogs. How can love be an action?

But real love has nothing to do with what I'm feeling. In fact, I may well feel the opposite of attraction to someone when I do something loving for them. The point is I do it anyway. I do it despite my anger or distaste. Because it is the kind and loving thing to do. The loving thing to do is pick up the phone when I don't feel like talking to a program person or *this* program person. The loving thing to do is offer to help when someone is going through a medical crisis, even if it means my to-do list waits. The loving thing to do is put my desires second, when someone else's needs should be first. It's not every time and it is not being a doormat. I know when what's being asked of me is the right thing to do, and when it isn't. It is the difference between God's will and mine.

Addiction Cycle   March 24

Work addiction is such a cruel cycle. I feel bad about myself for any number of reasons, so I work compulsively because I can make myself feel better by being productive and getting attention. Then I feel bad about myself because I've worked compulsively and didn't keep promises to myself and others. I tell myself I'm such a loser and have no self-control. Then I work compulsively again to make myself feel better.

Recovery is the beginning of the end of the cycle. As I listened to others work addicts, as I read the literature, as my sponsor gently reminded me it is the disease, not me, that is the problem, I began to short-circuit the endless repetition. I used my tools (meetings; telephone; sponsor; literature; prayer and meditation; writing; top and bottom lines; action plan; rest and relaxation; and service), first tentatively, then enthusiastically as I got results. I started to like who I saw in the mirror. I began to stop using work and productivity to make me feel like a worthwhile person. And that turns into a healthy, reinforcing cycle too.

Recovery Rooms   March 25

While there are many different 12-Step programs, every addiction does not have a room. In addition to a fiction reading addiction, I found social media and games on my phone can be addictive. Same with binge-watching shows. Other people are addicted to the Internet generally, surfing from one page to another, chasing one subject after another that grabs their attention. The Internet, fiction, games, shows, and social media are positive influences in our lives when used in moderation. Given enough spiritual bankruptcy, I can make anything an escape from doing what I should be doing or feeling my feelings.

The way I act out in my addiction is not important. The fact that I'm not willing to be present is the problem. I'm like a three-year-old having a tantrum, not wanting to take responsibility for my situation. It's an addiction problem when I find I'm powerless to keep promises to myself regarding my use of a given outlet or pastime, and it is causing me unmanageability, such as not being able to see to appropriate self-care or meet other responsibilities on my plate.

While it is helpful to have recovery rooms which address specific ways I act out, I find I can analogize tools from existing programs to cover those addictions for which a room doesn't exist (yet).

Surrender   March 26

If I recruit a new attorney to my law firm, I receive 2% of what the attorney makes at the firm, as long as we both stay. This can work out to be a lot more than the typical $5-10,000 most law firms offer their attorneys as a referral bonus. After being at my law firm for two years, I have brought in exactly one recruit.

This week, three new attorneys expressed interest in joining my firm. My brain went into overdrive. I was spending hours speaking with them, introducing them to others, researching their practices, obsessing about what could go wrong, counting my financial chickens before they laid golden eggs.

That is my disease. It is attracted to glittery new developments, particularly ones with dollar signs attached. It is so ambitious. How was I ever going to sleep?

I realized I needed to surrender this outcome. I needed to be okay with every one of those recruits not working out. Maybe they would decide my firm wasn't the right fit for them, maybe the firm would decide the candidates were not right for us. I had to be okay with the outcome. Once I got myself there, I could put in a normal effort around the candidates. I could stop thinking "I want what I want when I want it" and start focusing on being of service to my firm and my partners, existing and prospective. Even though I wanted to work over the weekend to keep advancing the recruiting ball, I kept telling myself it would keep until Monday morning, and then I could spend several hours on it if I wanted to. And that's what I did.

Before recovery, I happily gossiped about other people. I didn't see the problem. I loved the way gossip made me feel: superior and bonding with the person I was gossiping with, united against a common enemy. I continued to feel this way into my recovery. I heard people talking about gossiping—or character assassination—at meetings, but I wasn't willing to stop. Little by little, though, the nagging sense this too would have to go the way of my addictions was becoming evident. I began to try to not gossip. It was really hard. I was generally okay with not starting the gossip, but if someone else dropped a juicy tidbit and looked at me expectantly, I was dead meat.

This happened one day at work and I took the bait. I knew I'd made a mistake immediately. I went back to the person I gossiped with the next day, and said, "I'm sorry I said that thing about Laura yesterday. I'm trying not to talk negatively about people." Then, as an indirect amends I forced myself to take Laura to lunch. I couldn't do a direct amends because it would injure her if she knew what I'd said behind her back.

I asked around in meetings for suggestions to respond to other people gossiping. People suggested, "I'm sure they are doing the best they can," or simply, "Now, now."

It didn't seem like powerful magic but, you know, other people feel awkward when they drop a judgmental statement out there about a third party who isn't present, and no approval is forthcoming. No one wants to be the only one gossiping—it's a group sport. So those people who had come to expect me to gossip with them stopped trying. And then I didn't need to work so hard to avoid it.

One time, one of my siblings, A, said something negative to me about a family member, B. I suggested to A that they speak directly to B. That is the last time A gossiped with me. And since I've stopped gossiping among extended family members, my family has begun sharing with me their confidences, because they are comfortable it won't come back to bite them. What an amazing gift of the program I didn't come here looking for.

Surrender   March 28

One of my character defects is my incomplete surrender to my Higher Power. While I have taken the 3rd step and made a decision to turn my will and my life over to the care of my Higher Power, I snatch back my will in so many ways. Obsession, perfectionism, worry, control.

My Higher Power tells me: "This process is a continuum. You don't have to do it perfectly. Some surrender is better than none. You will want to surrender more as you see the benefits of surrendering some."

An affirmation I use to help me remember my third step decision: "I can do God's will all day; it will bring me joy."

Meditation   March 29

My first experience with meditation was in treatment. They gave us a Good 'n Plenty candy and told us to taste it for five minutes and keep bringing our thoughts back to it. As you can imagine, when I found myself in treatment, my life was a train wreck. Meditation gave me permission to stop analyzing for five minutes what a mess I'd made of my life.

One of the guys in treatment that night said the meditation wasted five minutes he could have been thinking about all the trouble in the world. I was ready, he wasn't. No judgment. When I was 23, I went to my first 12-Step meeting. I attended my second when I turned 40. My 23-year-old self wasn't ready. My 40-year-old self was. We all get here when it is time.

"God is never late." – 12-Step saying

Cunning, Baffling, and Powerful   March 30

How can having fewer things to get done make me crazier? I planned to go to Milwaukee for lunch with a new client on Friday. On Wednesday, the client cancelled because they had forgotten their office was closing early for Good Friday. So, I told my usual Friday sponsee I could meet with him after all because of the cancellation. Then Friday morning, my sponsee cancels. So, now God has cleared my Friday calendar twice and I was spinning about all the tasks I now think I can get done. I hadn't been obsessing before about the client

60

meeting or the sponsee meeting but opening a few hours in my calendar creates a Pandora's box of indecision.

I checked in with a program friend who was also struggling with her action plan for the day. We shared our ambitions for the day. We then proceeded—totally unplanned—to text each other after we completed one task after another on our to-do lists. We were both so satisfied with our sober accomplishments by 3:30, we could knock off and enjoy the weekend.

I've heard people at 12-Step meetings say, *"My mind is a dangerous neighborhood to walk in alone."* Thank goodness I have people to call who understand.

Substitution   March 31

We do not cram new tasks into our schedules; rather, we substitute by eliminating activities that demand equivalent time and energy. – The Workaholics Anonymous Book of Recovery, 2nd Edition, pp. 29-30.

Substitution has been an important tool for me in my recovery from workaholism. The idea is if a new commitment would take more than a few hours or extend over weeks or months, then before I accept it, I have to figure out what to give up.

Let's say someone asks me to sponsor them. My impulse in the past was to say "Yes." In fact, my AA program dictated that I "never say no to service." Also, my ego lights up when anyone asks me to be their sponsor. I love to rescue people, so I'm fighting an uphill battle to say no. It never occurred to me the time had to come from somewhere; that there wasn't any unending supply of time at my disposal.

A sponsoring commitment is at least 1-2 hours a week in the beginning and could entail time every week for years. With the tool of substitution, I ask myself, "What am I willing to give up? Family time? Work time? Self-care? Relaxation time? Sleep?"

Especially at the beginning of my workaholism recovery, I couldn't give up any of those things. I had mortgaged my time to the hilt and my sponsor encouraged me to get rid of commitments in my schedule. Thus, I located the word "no" in my repertoire. There is an immediate stab of guilt and disappointment when I say it, but later I'm relieved I didn't compromise my sobriety.

Resentment Inventory   April 1

As a WA sponsor, the first time I guide a sponsee through the 3rd column of the Step 4 resentment inventory, I suggest she identify what each resentment threatens for her with the following simple descriptions: physical security, emotional security, personal relations, sex relations, ambition, self-esteem or financial security. The first time through, it is enough the sponsee can identify her initial perceived threats.

If I'm working with my sponsee on inventorying current resentments, or she is going through the steps a second time, I encourage her to dig deeper in the third column. I glean so much self-awareness from this exercise.

For instance, if my husband is the subject of my resentment because he said something to make me angry, I can see a lot is threatened. His comment threatens my ambition because I want a happy and long-lasting marriage, and clearly if he is saying things to make me angry, we must get divorced. He threatens my financial security because if we get divorced, I won't live at the standard of living to which I am accustomed. He threatens my emotional security because all that divorce stuff will upset my equilibrium. Of course, his comment will mess up my personal relations with my kids because their father and I are no longer together. Finally, my sexual relations with my husband are affected because, well, we're not married any more.

All this, because he said something to make me angry. I ladder to a disproportionate state compared with the original offense. My emotional reaction will be off the charts. When I "right-size" the threat to what is going on in reality, I can ask myself "How important is it?" and mellow out. I have a better chance of responding appropriately to his comment if I don't think my very existence is hanging in the balance.

Pacing and Step 2   April 2

Step 2 says it will restore me to sanity. When I work under pressure, I cannot think as clearly. When I pace myself, try not to do too much in one stretch, and build in breaks, I can tap into resources that help me work smarter. Most of the stress in my day is self-imposed and imaginary. If I can catch myself feeling pressured, I can slow the pace and recover my sanity.

Core Beliefs   April 3

One of the first assignments my WA sponsor suggested was looking at my core beliefs, identifying their origin and challenging them. Here's my list:

1. *I believe I need to work to have value.*
2. *I believe not working means I'm lazy. Lazy is bad.*
3. *I believe a lot of my self-esteem comes from my accomplishments.*
4. *Depending on the task, I believe I'm competent.*
5. *Depending on the task, I believe I'm inadequate.*
6. *I believe I need other people's approval to be okay.*
7. *I believe financial dependence on another is unacceptable.*
8. *I believe to do the job right, I must do it myself.*
9. *I believe it is weakness to ask for help.*

Even after many years of recovery, I can look at this list and feel in my heart how each one of them still holds truth for me, and I can also understand in my head they are all wrong. We call them core beliefs because they appeared at an early and impressionable age. To mix a metaphor, it is difficult to swim against the current of my default wiring. But at least I can better understand and appreciate the enormity of the task when I see in black and white what I'm fighting. And I can be quicker to correct myself when I react from my core belief programming because I understand it lies to me.

Being Enough   April 4

I fear being inadequate which causes me to run away from challenges, especially public speaking in a professional context. But I can also hear the old tape of "you are not enough" in many situations, often just contemplating what I need to get done that day. It can paralyze me if I listen to its hypnotic persuasiveness.

My recovery has shown me if I run away, I will never learn *I am enough*. As uncomfortable as it is to stay and face the challenge, staying is the way I grow, and develop the skills I need to meet the demands of the next challenge. An affirmation I tell myself to counteract the deceptive voice of the addict is simply "I am enough."

Wherever I go, there I am. –12-Step slogan

Being of Service to Family   April 5

A guy at one of my 12-Step meetings says he asks his wife every morning what he can do to be of service to her. This blew my mind. I didn't believe I could ever make the same offer to my husband because I was afraid he would take advantage of me. I was sure he would ask me to do something time-consuming, leaving me without time to accomplish the tasks on my to-do list.

After hearing the guy at my meeting mention this for many years, I got up the nerve to try it. I felt so vulnerable and unprotected. My husband couldn't come up with anything. I asked again another day. I haven't made it a habit or anything, but this showed me, yet again, how I can be certain I know how something will go, and how wrong I can be.

Self-Care   April 6

I'm grateful today for a routine of self-care. In the midst of an insanely pressured workday, I went to the bathroom when I needed to, drank my water, ate my healthy meals and snacks, and got in 40 minutes of aerobic exercise. That is a miracle. Even without the other tools of WA, I have made a lot of progress against this disease just by bringing in the sanity and balance of self-care.

Diagnosing Work Addiction   April 7

I don't consider myself to be a textbook workaholic because I didn't spend 70 hours a week at a paying job, routinely miss dinner, or ruin my health and marriage because of my excessive working. I certainly conducted my life in other ways that qualify me as a work addict, such as working full-time at a stressful job while going to law school at night, and then doing a Masters program while working a stressful part-time job with two little kids at home, while my husband was working full time. And insisting on A's in all of my classes.

But because I never exhibited the classic signs or consequences of work addiction, diagnosis was elusive. Mostly it manifested in an excessive energy around work. I would wear out my friends and husband talking about work situations and colleagues. I took an intense interest in the outcome of my work efforts and acted as if everything hung in the balance. Failure was not an option.

Recovery has helped me right-size my attitudes with regard to work. When I'm feeling that intensity, I try to ask myself, "What's the worst that can happen if this doesn't go the way I think it should?" The answers are something like this:

-   "The client loses respect for me,"
-   "The client yells at me,"
-   "The client fires me," and
-   "I don't make the money that I should have made on the project."

Then, if I'm in good spiritual condition, I can usually get myself into acceptance of those situations, because I remember that the client is not my Higher Power. I remember, too, that this is not the only client, and I will have other opportunities to impress this client with my brilliance, if I remain sober and balanced throughout the process.

Shoulds   April 8

My sponsor suggested I make a list of the "shoulds" that I think I should do.

-   I should return calls right away.
-   I should make moves in Words with Friends immediately.
-   I should exercise three times a week.
-   I should call my mom on Sunday.
-   I should check Facebook every day.
-   I should post pictures of all the fun I'm having on Facebook often.
-   I should walk my dogs three times a day.
-   I should not go to work when my 15-year-old is home sick.
-   I should vote and take more of an interest in politics.
-   I should write more blogs for my work website.

Today, I'm grateful for the hope I have that it is okay to let myself off the hook for not doing everything I should. If I prioritize more, I can focus on the important or immediate items first and let other tasks slide.

Honesty and Steps 1, 2, and 3 April 9

I found honesty is something I've needed at every step in my recovery. One of my realizations since coming into recovery is the lack of honesty I exhibited in my life. There's the obvious dishonesty—like stealing. And then there's the subtler dishonesty—lying to myself, denying I'm an addict, not honestly evaluating my skills, not acknowledging the weaknesses of others, thinking I need to be perfect. My brain sends me a lot of messages that simply aren't true.

Working the steps has given me lots of opportunities to see my dishonesty. I have written a Step 1 around my work on multiple occasions. My addict would prefer I stay in denial as to my powerlessness and the unmanageability of my life. My addict wears blinders to the truth, and as long as I leave the blinders on, I remain in pain and obsession with my problems.

Steps 2 and 3 required me to quit lying to myself about how well self-reliance was working for me. Sure, I looked good on the outside with the career and family, but on the inside, I was a mess. When I took steps 2 and 3, however imperfectly, it was my honest admission I couldn't continue based on willpower anymore. I needed help from a power greater than myself.

Honesty and Steps 4 and 5 April 10

When I worked step 4, I saw how I had been dishonestly looking at my various situations and relationships as though I were a victim and had to just accept that. As my sponsor says, "*Victim is a volunteer position.*" I lacked the experience at those times in my life, and frequently today, to see the options available to me. For instance, when my practice group leader doesn't take care of the administrative things I need to run my practice, I go into self-pity and throw up my hands. When I'm forced to look at my dishonesty around this situation, I have to admit my practice group leader doesn't have the skills necessary to take the ball and run with administrative matters. I need to compensate for him. I could schedule time on his calendar to get him to focus on the issue. I could ask his permission to go over his head to get the approval, which he would willingly grant me because he hates this part of his job. This is new information for me: creative solutions to solve my problems that don't involve me feeling like a victim.

Another lie my 4th step revealed was the many times in my life my brain had told me I need X to be ok. X could be any number of things. For instance, it might be praise at work, the next academic degree, the next big client. My 4th step work showed me I'm being dishonest when I'm focused on getting something outside myself to make myself feel whole. The truth is, if I have a trusting connection to my Higher Power and try to do the next right thing, I'll be okay.

The 5th step is primarily honesty. I needed to get honest with one person—my sponsor—and tell her all there was to know about my deepest secrets.

Honesty and Steps 6 and 7   April 11

In Steps 6 and 7, I had to take an honest look at my character defects and try to figure out which ones were killing me enough to ask God to remove them. I wish I could say I identified my flaws and I'm willing to let God take them all, but I'm not there yet. This is a step I need to keep working on. As the addictive acting out has stopped, I am given an opportunity to live life on life's terms. This means I have to live my life over time in order for the defects to surface. I interact with other humans, deal with problems, go to work and confront changes. Then my defects come out to play. I get a chance to do steps 1-3 around them and surrender yet another one. But it happens in God's time, not mine. If I'm not being killed by a character defect today, I'll hold onto it for a while longer, thank you very much.

Honesty and Steps 8 and 9   April 12

In steps 8 & 9, I made a list of the people I harmed and tried to make it up to them. My list contained people I had stolen from. I didn't appreciate the severity of my dishonesty problem until I faced the numbers in my 8th and 9th steps. The items I stole were mostly not valuable, but I stole little things often. I had to go back to people, admit my dishonesty and pay them back. I have to admit I didn't feel much hardship in repaying people because I had adequate funds. However, the humility I needed to muster to admit it was monumental. My ego was screaming at me to stop. But what my ego wants was irrelevant; I realized in order to obtain the rewards in this program, I needed to clean up the wreckage of my past and right the wrongs. I needed to keep doing the next right thing.

We talk about doing the next right thing, and sometimes it is not obvious. But I can be sure I'm on the right track if I don't do the next wrong thing, like lying, cheating, and stealing.

I needed honesty in working step 9. My ego is so big. It tells me my amends are a big deal to the people I'm making them to. That my amends have to be perfect. Better not make them yet; they aren't perfect yet. That there's no hurry, there's no deadline, I can wait until tomorrow and that will present the perfect opportunity to make the amends. That's my addict talking and my addict lies. The reality is my amends are fine, just the way they are. And now is the right time to make my amends, so I continue moving forward in the steps. My addict hates the discomfort I feel before making an amends. But the cool part is, once I make the amends, I enjoy huge relief and joy at how it went.

Honesty and Step 10   April 13

In Step 10, I write a nightly inventory. This is an opportunity for me to keep my act clean as I go. I look through my day and note the highlights. It gives me a chance for introspection which is new for me. I notice I'm ticked off at someone, or I feel bad about something. Before, I would have ignored those feelings because they make me uncomfortable, and I'm a feel-good junkie. Now, the 10th step forces me to be more honest. I make a mental note to apologize in real time, instead of waiting to do a 4th step in the future. I make a mental note to confront somebody if I think it necessary. Taking care of these issues as they come up prevents them from building up in me and exploding and making me act out in self-destructive ways.

Honesty and Step 11   April 14

In Step 11, I get to daily right-size myself. You see, my ego and addict wants me to be important, wants me to think my agenda is the way events should unfold. This is a lie. I'm not important in the big scheme of things. I forget that all the time. In Step 11, I pray and meditate and recommit myself daily, and sometimes by the minute, to ascertaining what God wants me to do, and doing it. It doesn't matter what I want. And I get amazing relief from this little revelation.

Honesty and Step 12   April 15

Step 12 tells me I get to practice these principles in all my affairs. My problem was I didn't know how to deal with *any* of my affairs, so I hid. Whenever life threw me a curveball or an emotion, I escaped with grandiosity and obsession and hits of praise from co-workers. Take away my addictive behavior, and I'm forced to face my life. I thought my life would be too bland without adding the extra spice of working addictively. But that was a lie from my addict intended to keep me in bondage. My life is far from bland. Sure, there are chores I would prefer to ignore, but I find when I do the next right thing, it's done and I still have my self-respect and maybe a sense of accomplishment. I receive amazing benefits from finding a Higher Power to direct me and relying on my Higher Power. The input I receive from people in program to help me solve my problems means I'm continually learning and thriving, and it feels great. And I'm a feel-great junkie, so I'll keep coming back.

Surrender   April 16

In the last month, four attorneys contacted me and expressed an interest in joining my law firm. Instead of a finder's fee at my firm, I receive 2% of my recruits' collections for as long as we are both at the firm. This can add up to a significant supplement to my legal work if I bring in enough candidates. I found myself calculating how much money that could be. I contemplated, after work hours, what additional information I might forward to them to show my firm in the best light and make them want to join us. I worried one of my partners would interview my recruits, say the wrong thing and turn them off. When I'm in my disease, I'm selfish, controlling and obsessive.

It finally occurred to me I had to surrender the entire outcome. So many factors play into whether a person gets offered or takes a given job. My Higher Power told me my job is simply to make the introductions and keep the ball rolling so if it is meant to be, it happens. My Higher Power told me my job is to ascertain what is in the best interests of these attorneys, my firm and our clients. I was so much happier once I surrendered my need for these attorneys to join my firm. I could just enjoy the process.

Admitting Mistakes   April 17

Well into recovery, one day I was trying to set up a meeting at work. I made a mistake with the time zones, as I am wont to do, potentially scheduling myself into two conflicting meetings. When I realized my mistake, I emailed my client, implying he had waited too long to book the openings I gave him and indicating my available time was now narrower. It occurred to me later that day I needed to make amends because I had lied.

I emailed the client, admitting both my mistake with the time zones and the subsequent lie to cover it up. It was a humbling email to send.

To this day, that client thinks I walk on water. I guess he figures if I got an attack of conscience over such a small matter, well, I just must be the most trustworthy attorney he knows.

Mistakes don't disqualify me from the human race; they validate my entry form. —my sponsor

Inactivity   April 18

I identify in WA meetings as a "work and activity addict." That means I not only make myself crazy with my paid work, but also with non-stop activities of life. These include service, social, political, physical, leisure—you name it, nothing is safe. The crux of my workaholism is my "dis-ease" with a lack of activity. If there's always something going on, I am comfortable and don't have to feel or think about uncomfortable topics. I'm always on the go.

Here's an example from my journal early in WA recovery:

"When I got home from work, I had 45 minutes to make and eat dinner, get dinner ready for my youngest and I pushed myself to accomplish other tasks, such as recording a bunch of events on the family calendar and paying bills. I drove my youngest to Girl Scouts, and when it turned out they didn't need me to stay, instead of going home and relaxing, I went clothes shopping. Granted, I really *needed* clothes, but I pushed myself to go to not one but two stores. And I was multitasking on my phone while driving and again later when I was making (burning) popcorn. And I couldn't take five minutes to meditate."

Therefore, and ironically in our culture, I celebrate it as an accomplishment when I choose to do nothing. This takes many forms, such as:

- meditation;
- not checking my email or other media when I have a few moments;
- sitting in front of a fire;
- listening to music and not doing anything else while listening;
- getting a massage;
- allowing a break in the conversation;
- taking a hot bath; or
- listening to my body just enough to realize that a nap is in order, and then actually taking a nap.

Don't just do something, sit there – from an Alanon meeting

The Iceberg   April 19

When I came into recovery, I thought my acting out behaviors were the problem. If I stopped acting out, I would be fine. However, the visible behaviors (for instance, frantic activity, jockeying for position, talking about work constantly, over-committing my time and not taking breaks) were just the tip of the iceberg. The tip is all that can be seen of an iceberg. There's a whole lot going on beneath the water. So it was with my disease. Ninety-five percent of the problem was invisible and encompassed the underlying causes and conditions that set the stage for my acting out. Addressing the visible behaviors was only a small part of the solution. The real work would be on the hard stuff: the fears, ambition, jealousy, low self-esteem, dishonesty, selfishness and other character defects. I acted out with the visible behaviors because I needed to numb out from pain caused by the crap beneath the surface. If I didn't have the crap, I wouldn't need to escape into my addictions.

Recovery has given me the blow torches and pick axes I need to address my iceberg, should I care to pick them up. They include the following principles: honesty, courage, service, humility, self-awareness, love, tolerance, faith, patience, gratitude, compassion, kindness, gentleness, self-care, minding my own business, trying new alternatives and looking at my choices.

Rest **April 20**

We check our level of energy before proceeding to our next activity.—The Workaholics Anonymous Book of Recovery, 2nd Edition, p. 30.

This idea never occurred to me before I joined WA. If the task appeared on the schedule, I did it. As long as there remained waking hours in the day, I proceeded to the next activity. I gave no consideration to my physical, mental, or emotional availability for the task. There wasn't even a pause between one task and the next for such an energy-level check to occur.

Now, I try to schedule 15 minutes between one meeting and the next. The break allows me to use the bathroom, get more (decaf) coffee, check my email, reconsider and re-prioritize my to-do list for the rest of the day. This prevents elevation of my adrenalin and keeps me in reality as to what is coming. I have more intuitive, time-saving flashes about how to proceed, rather than just pushing forward mindlessly. My days are much calmer.

Making Amends **April 21**

I thought making amends would be awkward, humiliating, and pointless. I was willing to go through with it only to complete my step work.

It was only once I had made a few amends, I began to understand the value of this process. First, it allows me to go through life with less perfectionism. I don't have to get everything right the first time: I can come back and clean up if I make mistakes. What a profound shift in my worldview this is. I can go a little more easily, a bit happier, less weighed down.

Second, when I screw things up with other people and treat them badly, amends give me a chance to set the record straight. You see, when I screw up, until I make amends, the other person could conclude I believe my behavior is okay, and I am crazy. If I tell the other person, "Jeez, that thing I did or said? I was wrong. I don't know what I was doing." So now the other person realizes, "Oh, thank God, she's not really crazy." Thus, I benefit from making amends. My reputation improves. Amends are actually image management put to good purpose.

Work fears

Going into today, I was afraid because an important client requested a meeting. What did he want to discuss? Was he upset with our service? Did I over-promise?

I tried to manage my fear in the moment with mental admonitions, positive self-talk and affirmations:

(1) it is not time to think about you now, you can wait until I get to work;

(2) God will take care of me;

(3) I'm better at this kind of conversation than I give myself credit for; and

(4) how can I be of service to my client, instead of worrying about how I will look.

Turns out, my fear was unfounded and the discussion went fantastically. The client was happy with our work and wanted to give us more similar work. I even followed it up with another home run by picking up on the client's hint concerning a different area in which he could use support and offered to help there, which he accepted.

My disease lies to me.

Sleeplessness

The night is the hardest time to be alive and 4am knows all my secrets. —Poppy Z. Brite

I have struggled with sleep. I'm protective of my sleep. I spent many years addicted to Sominex. When I'm awake in the middle of the night and unable to fall back asleep, I get worried I won't have what it takes the next day. That makes me more uptight and unable to relax. Problems loom larger in the middle of the night when I'm alone with my thoughts. Tools that help me fall asleep are meditation or saying the Serenity Prayer over and over, like a mantra.

Sometimes my sleeplessness is not due to a particular problem. Sometimes it is free-floating anxiety. In that case, I remind myself I'm powerless over my sleep. It is not in my power to make myself fall asleep—only my Higher Power can do it. My job is to make the conditions optimal so sleep might happen. I need to be in bed, eyes closed, no music, no light, no caffeine. Relaxed and not willing myself to fall asleep. Just telling myself it is not my concern whether I fall asleep; I have done my job to make the conditions right. This takes the pressure off me, and paradoxically allows sleep to creep in.

Using People   April 24

One of my shortcomings is using other people to make me feel good about myself. For instance, I was a "teacher's pet" in school because I loved getting attention from authority figures. I might go above and beyond to provide excellent service to bosses, partners and clients solely to get praise and approval. I am often not motivated to provide good service because I care about the outcome for the client. Using other people for how they make me feel is the opposite of loving them and being of service to them.

Recovery has shown me that by using people in this way, I deprive them of my being present to the relationship. I don't need their affirmation to be ok. It is only temporary and superficial compared to the joy I can attain if I look to my Higher Power for approval.

An affirmation I can use to help me when I forget: "I don't need other people's attention to be okay. God's attention, approval and love are ever-present."

Accepting Help   April 25

As I've mentioned, an inability to ask for help is one symptom of my workaholism. I must always appear competent. When I got sick with cancer, many people offered to help. I had no idea how to accept such help, or even where to begin. I had two young children at home and a household to run, although I'd taken a two-month leave of absence from work. Of course, my husband was supportive and covering all kinds of extra bases. But it was just too much for one person, and I was in real danger of over-exerting myself too soon after surgery. One of my sponsees stepped up to show me how to do service for a sick person. She asked me to funnel all offers of help to her. She made up a chart of every day for the first month, and enlisted people to bring dinner to my house each night. It was amazing. Not only did it lighten our load for grocery shopping and food prep, but I visited with people for fifteen minutes or so when they dropped off dinner, at a time when I couldn't get out to recovery meetings.

I have since picked up the service chart organizer role for people in my life who have had medical difficulties. In addition to organizing dinners, I signed up people to do tasks such as drive the sick person to doctor appointments, get groceries, clean the litter box, walk the dog, or just visit. I am inspired by how willing people are to help but often the person needing help doesn't know how to organize it. Or it is too hard to ask for help. Having the go-between of a clearinghouse person to match needs with resources is an amazingly helpful role, and one that can be done sitting at a computer.

There will be times in my life when I can't do it all, and times other people can't either. This is one way to help and to accept help that allows us to gracefully survive the curveballs life sometimes throws.

How I Spend my Time   April 26

In early WA recovery, as I continued to log my hours on an activity chart, I began to get objectivity as to how I spent my time. I saw I spent more time with my family than I thought and I didn't spend as much time with sponsees. I began to understand it didn't matter so much *what* I spent my time doing, as *how*. My discomfort is evident when I allow myself to feel pressured—put upon by external circumstances and wound up, feeling like I have to react. That can as easily be in my kitchen as at my desk. Just one more thing. Doing because people ask, not because it is the next right thing for me to be doing. I need more thoughtfulness about what I should do and less autopilot acceptance it is mine to do. My problem is I perceive everything as my job: at work, at home and in recovery. It's the reverse of that old cop out "It's not *my* job."

It helps to ask myself: Does something need to be done? Does something need to be done right now? Does something need to be done right now by me?

Media Time Out   April 27

I take a late afternoon walk with my dog to a coffee shop (for a caffeine-free latte), about 45 minutes round trip. Recently, on such a walk, I listened to a podcast on the way there, and chatted with a friend on the phone on the way home. Later, I wondered why I felt sadly unrefreshed and worn out. I realized that I had missed my quiet time on my walk. I vowed to try to make that walk a media-free zone. It nourishes me to spend it being grateful and present. Notice the weather, smell the flowers, feel how good it is to be able to walk, appreciate how silly my dog is, and how in-the-moment she is. I'm not 100% at ignoring media on my walks—work emails are particularly persistent at breaking in—but I strive for a B+ average for the week. Progress, not perfection.

No End to Recovery   April 28

Go to 90 meetings in 90 days. If you're not satisfied, we'll gladly refund your misery. —AA slogan

When I came into the rooms of recovery, I thought and hoped I might get help with my addictions. I had no idea how much more was in store for me. Not only did I stop acting out in my addictions, but I got help with my fear, anxiety, relationships, work problems, emotional problems, and dealing with difficult people in my life. I often hear people in the rooms say God has given them so much more than what they could imagine for themselves. Therefore, today I can only hope I continue to be motivated to do what recovery asks of me (step work, inventory, prayer and meditation, service, meetings, phone calls, amends, surrendering my will, self-care) one day at a time for the rest of my life, so I keep getting the good stuff.

Newcomer: *How long do I have to go to meetings?*
Old timer: *Until you want to go to meetings.*

Worry   April 29

Sometimes in my youth I can remember thinking "I have absolutely nothing hanging over my head and I'm not worried about anything." These moments were noteworthy because of their infrequency, and the lightness was so foreign, and delicious. Otherwise, I was always anxious. I wish I could say that today I feel that carefree all the time, but I'm not there yet.

I understand now how I use worry like a drug. It puts a barrier between me and God. When I'm concerned I won't get something I want (for instance, to be on time) then I'm not trusting that everything is the way it's supposed to be. I'm willing my will—by sheer force of my powerful worrying—onto the world around me. Onto cars and those in my company, I infect my kids with my worry instead of showing them how to do what we can control and then trust we'll be taken care of.

I can have nothing going on, and I will obsess over the smallest detail of some situation, just to worry about something. I guess the progress I've made on this front is my awareness of my dis-ease. When I catch myself obsessing over some trivial matter, I say to myself, "Oh, there's that thing I do again; my disease is alive and well, I see. God, please let me relax and not sweat the small stuff."

First Three Steps   April 30

It is said that a simple way to express the first three steps is "*I can't. God can. I think I'll let God.*"

So, let me make this more complicated.

Step 1:   "I can't." I'm powerless to stop my (a) compulsive working, (b) work fears and (c) obsessions about work with my own devices, and my life has become unmanageable.

Step 2:   "God can." Through witnessing the recovery of other workaholics, and slowly experimenting by taking suggestions and witnessing my own tenuous steps forward in recovery, I came to believe that a power greater than myself could restore me to sanity.

Step 3:   "I think I'll let God." I made a decision to turn my thoughts about how my work life should go and my work activities over to the care of a Higher Power.

I have to keep coming back to these steps over and over. Sometimes I can take them in a given situation and sometimes I'm powerless and willful. I notice though that things go better when I keep it simple and just take them.

Step 5   May 1

Step 5 says: We admitted to God, to ourselves and to another person the exact nature of our wrongs.

The 5th step was hard for me. There were things on my 4th step list I wasn't sure I could bring myself to say out loud. Things I had never told anyone. I considered taking the half-measure of admitting most of my wrongs but keeping the worst ones to myself. I didn't want my sponsor to know these things about me. I valued her opinion of me, and I thought she would be disgusted by me if she heard the truth.

I heard from my sponsor and others in recovery that if I kept the worst secrets to myself, I would continue to harbor shame, and that's what my addict feeds on. As my sponsor says, "I was either in this or I wasn't." I couldn't come up with any better ideas. I would be hurting my progress in the program if I didn't come clean. I arrived at my 5th step meeting full of resolve and certain, at the end of the day, I would have this behind me. God had other plans. We spent seven hours going over my resentment inventory, and didn't get to the fear inventory, where I had written the humiliating incidents. Now it seemed I must wait another week until we met for another 7 hours to finish my 5th step.

So, I came back the following week and we made it through. When I got to the hard stuff, my sponsor not only accepted what I said without judgment, but she told me how she had done something similar. I felt light leaving that meeting: forgiven and washed clean. I know now that what I did took honesty, courage and humility. These are virtues I value, and knowing I did this step to the best of my ability increases my self-esteem, which is the antidote to my addiction.

Stay afraid, but do it anyway. What's important is the action. You don't have to wait to be confident. Just do it and eventually the confidence will follow. –Carrie Fisher

Relaxing and Step 2   May 2

When I feel pressure, instead of believing the lie it tells me that I have to work harder and faster, I need to do the opposite and stop working. It is counter-intuitive. But working under the pressure is insanity. I am cut off from God and in complete self-will. When I relax, I'm able to better see God's will for me and the path to sanity.

Came to believe that a Power greater than ourselves could restore us to sanity. – Step 2

Lying   **May 3**

I surprised myself with my character defects this week. Last Friday, which happened be Good Friday, a new client asked me to handle a big project for them. I didn't have relevant experience, but I knew lawyers who did. I set out to pick their brains. I emailed two former partners of mine at the same law firm, posed my questions and dangled the project in front of them, assuming they wouldn't talk to each other, because I knew they weren't close. My goal was to gather as much information as quickly as I could, to impress the client. Larry called me back and helped me think it through. Greg, the other partner, forwarded my email to Larry, copying me, saying it was more within Larry's bailiwick. I felt caught and embarrassed. I quickly covered and emailed, "Great minds think alike. I just spoke with Larry. I didn't know who I would find in the office this Good Friday between Spring breaks." Thing is, that was a convenient excuse, but it never occurred to me when I reached out to them.

In my nightly inventory, I noted discomfort with the situation. And promptly forgot about it. Five days later, I prepared an agenda for my check-in with my sponsor, going through my inventory writing, and I made a note to discuss it with her. That was when it hit me: I might owe them an amends. Fuck no, I'm not making an amends. What was the harm? I used them for their expertise, and I *lied* to them to cover up why I asked them separately. Oh God, I need to make amends. I sent the following email to them:

"Hi guys—I'm writing to apologize for my behavior on Friday. I wrote to each of you separately, thinking the more input I got and sooner on my problem, the smarter I would appear to the client. Then I lied to cover it up by attributing it to Good Friday vacations. I didn't want to look bad. So sorry to treat you that way. I hope you will not think too badly of me and that we will again be able to work together on something. In fact, I have given Larry's name to the client and they are considering how to staff."

Of course, they were both gracious. I was glad I cleaned it up, but irritated I could (a) still, after years of recovery, be so blinded by my ambition I use people this way, (b) have a lie roll off my tongue (keyboard) so quickly and easily I didn't know I'd done it and (c) have it take five days for me to realize what I'd done. It's not like I'm unaware of this character defect of lying. I ask God every morning in my prayers to help me "not lie to make myself look better."

The good news is I have the tools today to help me straighten these things out eventually: self-awareness, 10th step, sponsor check-in, amends, humility, courage.

Fear of Public Speaking   May 4

I'm afraid of speaking in public, particularly in work situations. I worry I will make mistakes, look silly and not be smooth enough, or not appear to be an expert.

As part of my 6th step work, my sponsor suggested that I ask God about this, and here is what I heard: "I gave you above average intelligence, a sense of humor, enthusiasm, articulateness and a personality that others find attractive. I also gave you an opportunity to earn three degrees, so you are well-educated. You are pleasant enough to look at. You have computer skills to create effective presentations. There is nothing stopping you but yourself."

As a result, I try to accept reasonable opportunities to share my gifts. An affirmation I tell myself when I'm feeling troubled is "I have valuable insights to offer. I am articulate."

Letter to God: 3:18 am   May 5

Dear God:

I just realized all of the files and emails for the Marque X portfolio which are being shipped to me may be in French. I don't know French. I've never taken over a portfolio from a French firm before. I guess I was being cocky and making assumptions about English. I don't know what to do next. I'm scared to tell the client and I'm scared to get 50 boxes of documents I can't understand. It's overwhelming enough to take in a portfolio of this size in English. I'm scared to be stuck paying translation and scanning costs. I'm scared I'm going to have 50 boxes in my dining room for years because I can't even interpret them enough to put them in filing cabinets. Please help me trust I will be okay and you will provide me the guidance and resources I need.

I have had problems at work before that seemed insurmountable because I can't understand how to resolve them, and eventually they get resolved. I know in a month, this problem will not be haunting me because it will have been addressed one way or another. What's the worst that can happen? I don't get the client after all and I lose face with my former colleague who hired me. I won't be in much worse shape than I was two weeks ago, when this wasn't my client yet. My discomfort comes from my fear of losing something I have. I'm in selfish mode here. Not thinking at all of how I can be of service to my client or my firm. One possible solution is to keep the current French firm on board. They can handle the French trademarks, and also keep the files. Whenever I need something from the files, I can ask them to provide it in English.

It is not lost on me the moment I started not thinking selfishly and being consumed with what I might lose, a creative viable solution appeared. I proposed the solution to the client the next day and they were fine with it. I got to keep the client, despite my imperfections.

Action Plan   May 6

A good day. I woke up with all kinds of ideas about what I could do today: work out, get my nails done, meet with two sponsees, get hours of work done, pick up my youngest at 2:45 from school and drive to their basketball game at another school, and then meet my dad and stepmom for dinner. Thank God I sat down with a pad and pen before I started anything and drew up a plan. I even listed taking a shower and having lunch.

It became evident many items had to go. The workout, manicure and hours of work moved to the next day. I got through the step work and sponsee meetings and a small bit of priority work, my kid's basketball game and dinner. I even allowed for some leisure reading and a nap. What a different outcome than my original ideas. I didn't feel pressured, inadequate, overwhelmed, or disappointed. I felt sane and measured and that I had met my priorities.

Being Wrong   May 7

There is a principle which is a bar against all information, which is proof against all arguments and which cannot fail to keep a man in everlasting ignorance—that principle is contempt prior to investigation.— Herbert Spencer

I started to notice sushi becoming popular in my 20's, but I never tried it because I was certain I wouldn't like it. This seemed so clear to me and I held sushi in contempt. Shortly after I got into recovery at age 40, I tried sushi. Turns out, I sought out sushi on many occasions going forward. How could I have been so wrong? How could I have not even investigated in order to determine the truth of the thing?

Just one of many examples of this in my recovery. I came across the above quote from Spencer in the AA Big Book, in the Appendix on Spiritual Experience. Like so many, I was so sure God didn't exist, and felt contempt for weak people who needed to believe in a Higher Power. Yet again, I was wrong. Sure is humbling to be so confident in my intellect, and regularly find I can't rely on it.

Work Addiction   May 8

Workaholism recovery has short-circuited the cycle of addiction that tells me I'm not enough and I need to do more to be ok. How uncomfortable it was to imagine myself a worker among workers...just another bozo on the bus. And yet, what a relief. The gentle messages in the WA literature that it was ok to stop striving for the sake of striving and just be okay with turning in a fair day's work for a day's pay. The surrender of my job as being "my" show, and looking at it instead as a group effort, was a paradigm shift. Asking myself what was in the best interests of my client, of my firm, of my partners? Instead of always focused on "What's in it for *me*?" and "How will this make *me* look?" It has made me a better partner and a better attorney.

Prayer   May 9

In early recovery, my sponsor suggested I pray on my knees out loud, twice a day, and I've been doing that although I miss from time to time.

I don't believe God needs to hear my prayers, because he knows them already. Rather, I need to hear them to remind myself of my areas of weakness and intentions to do things differently despite my default wiring.

Much of my morning prayer consists of asking for help with character defects identified in my 6th step work. It doesn't address all of my defects, but those I'm feeling acute pain from and I'm finally willing to do something about. Many of them are compulsive—things I do I'm powerless over, like blurting out unsolicited advice, lying to make myself look better or thinking judgmental thoughts. God knows my struggles with these, and I'm not telling him about them for his benefit. The point of me asking out loud for help with them in the morning is by heightening my awareness about my powerlessness about them, I gain the smallest possibility maybe when I need the extra second later in my day to not act compulsively, I will have the grace to do things differently.

A good day is when my actions match my intentions.

Morning Anxiety   May 10

For a long time, I suffered from morning anxiety. Every work morning, I felt pressure about the work on my desk. I was sure there wasn't enough time (how will I get it all done?) and/or that it is too hard for me (I'm not smart enough to solve the problems, no matter how many hours I work on it).

Despite the anxiety, through sheer willpower, I put one foot in front of the other and did the next right thing. At the end of the day, I had addressed everything that was critical, although I may have carried several non-urgent tasks to the next day. Nevertheless, I woke up the next morning with the same anxiety and the cycle repeated.

I prayed about it. God told me to look to previous work experiences where I have applied sober principles to overcome fear and discomfort. So, I looked at five work situations which required either:

(a)   delegating,

(b)   moderating my perfectionism,

(c)   asking for help,

(d)   making an outline of a complex job,

(e)   managing my own and other's expectations, prioritizing, or

(f)   focusing on service instead of my self-obsession.

God also directed me to read through the tools of Workaholics Anonymous to see what applied, and to read through my step work around work addiction to find any analogies. The relevant tools were to be Relaxing, Concentrating and Pacing. I wrote how each applied to my morning anxiety. After doing that work, my morning anxiety disappeared, and for the most part it has stayed away. When I notice it creeping in again, I re-read my written work and remind myself I'm still powerless and that seems to help.

Changing Careers   May 11

I worked in large law departments and big law firms for twenty-three years after law school. I was a partner at one of the largest international law firms in the world—1800 lawyers. I had a cushy salary and didn't have to work very hard, because I couldn't find enough work at $600-$800 an hour the firm charged for my services. I spent most of my time marketing and doing administrative work on the matters my associates did the legal work for.

After six years in recovery for work addiction, I realized I was bored, so I joined a virtual law firm of 30 partners. Everyone works from home. There are no associates or secretaries. No help desk for technology support. The partners do everything for themselves. There is no salary. It is entirely entrepreneurial—I only get paid for the work I do and collect from my clients. It is refreshing and terrifying. I have so enjoyed learning the technology required to run a law practice from home. I love getting my hands dirty doing the legal work myself and working directly with the clients again. I like not working for "the man." I love working from home and not having to get dressed and commute into the city. I work an average of twenty-five hours a week. I charge $350 an hour and my clients love it. I make the same money I did at the big law firm. I don't miss my nice office view. I don't care that no one recognizes the name of my firm. My dogs sleep on the floor at my feet.

When I went into recovery for work addiction, I defined myself by being a partner at a well-known firm. I was afraid "they" would make me quit my high-status partnership. Through the grace of my Higher Power and working the program, my priorities have changed and I'm a happier person for it.

Emotions   May 12

I attend a meditation class once a week, for 1½ hours. We experiment with different types of meditating. Today, we were in the part of the curriculum which shows us how to meditate with emotions. When I got to class, I didn't have any idea I was avoiding any emotions. It wasn't until we had meditated an hour and fifteen minutes that the tears came streaming down my face. I was thinking about my youngest who is going away to college this Fall in another state, who is getting tattoos on their wrists regardless of my concerns, who just told me they were bisexual, and who is attending a school with a party reputation, when they have never been drunk.

Now, I do have a son who is gay and I'm thrilled for my kids discovering their sexual identities. It is not being gay or bi *per se* that concerns me, but as a parent, I'm cognizant of the greater hardships in our culture queer people face. So, I worry about what they have in store. Apparently, I have a few emotions about situations they will be facing.

One of the reasons I act out with workaholism is because feelings are too painful. I would rather numb out and get hits from the illusion of control I derive from work. I'm not good at knowing when I have emotions brewing. And ignoring them or not giving them the respect they deserve can cause them to come out sideways in a way that is not good for my relationships or my health. Focusing on emotions during meditation is one way to encourage myself to feel my feelings.

"Feelings are like little kids: you can't keep them in a trunk, but you can't let them drive, either." –heard at a 12-Step meeting

Teasing   May 13

My workaholism is a lot about image management. I want to be respected and popular. One of the ways people know they are popular is because they are teased or roasted. Teasing is a two-edged sword. Depending on how it is intended and received, it can be a bad or good thing. There are certain subjects which I don't mind being teased at all about, like, for instance, my lack of math skills. I'm comfortable with this character defect, and in acceptance about it. There are other subjects, however, like my belly fat, which would not make me happy to be teased about.

When my family makes fun of my math skills, I know it is because they love me and feel comfortable enough with me they can show their love in this fun way. I try to be careful about teasing someone to make sure it is about a foible they aren't triggered around, before I let loose with the affection.

Emotional Sobriety   May 14

In 1958, Bill Wilson, the founder of Alcoholics Anonymous, wrote an article called "The New Frontier: Emotional Sobriety." Even after an alcoholic stops drinking, they often still struggle with a crippling excess of emotion. Bill Wilson attributes this in part to adolescent urges for top approval and perfect security from which we never matured. He notes, "How painful it is to keep demanding the impossible." I found his descriptions of this experience to mirror my workaholism.

He found that emotional sobriety could be lost by "a dependence on people or circumstances to supply me with prestige, security, and the like. Failing to get these things according to my perfectionist dreams and specifications, I had fought for them. And when defeat came, so did my depression." He defined dependency as a demand for "control of the people and the conditions surrounding me."

Bill Wilson also offered a ray of hope. "If I could rid myself of these dependencies, then I would be free to love unconditionally, and enjoy the serenity that I so desperately wanted." He gives an example of sponsoring someone in a 12-Step program. "The sponsor pours love and attention on a sponsee, who may ultimately not get any better. Rather than be frustrated at the lack of apparent success, the sponsor wishes the sponsee well and moves on to the next sponsee. There is no expectation of a given result, success, sobriety, gratitude or reciprocation. It is just an acceptance of the situation."

"If we examine every disturbance we have, great or small, we will find at the root of it some unhealthy dependency and its consequent unhealthy demand. Let us, with God's help, continually surrender these hobbling demands. Then we can be set free to live and love; we may then be able to Twelfth Step ourselves and others into emotional sobriety."

Speeding   May 15

One time I drove to Michigan from Chicago, for a golf outing for one of my clients. My partners and I had agreed to meet at 9 am. It wasn't until I got in the car, with plenty of time to make the two-hour drive, I realized I'd forgotten that Michigan is one hour ahead of Chicago. I spent the next two hours driving over ninety mph to make up the difference. I can now see my selfishness. I didn't care how an accident would mess up other people on the road. All I cared about was not looking stupid in front of my partners and clients. I should have called one of my partners and explained the problem and told them I'd be there an hour late. Today, one of my bottom lines is to drive no more than ten miles over the speed limit.

Wasting Time   May 16

Lately I've been noticing a lot of fighting-the-clock behavior. I will be working away on my to-do list and I'll look up and be shocked at the time. Or shocked it's already the 16th of May—where did the month go? I get so annoyed with wasted time.

I can't be bothered to go shopping—a pastime many people find enjoyable—but for me it involves wasted time driving to a mall, walking around trying to find things, trying clothes on. Why would I do that when I can just spend ten minutes on my computer and have it delivered? My husband asked if I wanted to go to the flower store with him and pick out annuals for our garden. I told him no because it was the weekend, the store would be crowded and we would waste so much time; I could go on a weekday instead. My disease prevented me from seeing how it might be a pleasurable way to spend quality time together.

I'm always looking for ways to combine errands: when I needed to pick up medicine at the vet, I told them I would swing by on Friday when I was going to be out that direction for a meeting. And don't even get me started about being stuck in traffic.

These situations which my disease deems to be wasteful could be opportunities for me to connect with my Higher Power. Instead of thinking "I'm losing productivity," I could be thinking "I'm gaining spirituality." I'll keep coming back.

Feelings   May 17

When I came into recovery, I hadn't cried in ten years. I didn't think I was afraid of anything. I heard people in treatment talking about fear, and I didn't know what they were talking about. I couldn't identify one single thing I was afraid of. One counsellor in treatment gave me a sheet with a bunch of different faces and emotions on it. I recognized maybe four feelings out of twenty I had ever felt.

Once I stopped acting out in my addictive behaviors I had utilized to escape from anything uncomfortable, I turned into a big raw nerve. Everything made me cry. I came to find out I'm afraid of everything.

One of my sponsors said feelings are simply information. I don't have to act on them. But they provide information to help me determine what I need to do. If I stuff them, they will come out sideways.

I often still don't recognize my feelings immediately. That is why a daily inventory is important for me. It gives me an opportunity away from the action of the day to reflect upon the events and my reaction to them. I can name what I was or am still feeling. I can then use a tool of the program to deal with the feelings, perhaps calling my sponsor, or writing a more thorough inventory about it.

Suicide   May 18

I know two people in the recovery rooms who committed suicide, and both were lawyers like me. John ended his life a few years ago, never having discovered WA, although I believe workaholism killed him. Anna died today.

John worked for the Securities Exchange Commission and his management assigned him to a trial he feared he was not competent to handle. The trial had a high profile. John hadn't handled a trial in 15 years. He talked about the situation in many meetings of a different fellowship. It doesn't matter what kind of addict we identify as; we discuss our fears in all the rooms of recovery. Eventually, the fear became too much and he walked into Lake Michigan.

After three years of abstinence from her addictions, Anna had a slip which led to the end of her marriage. After that, she stopped going to meetings and calling her sponsor. She became active in her addictions. She got more and more sketchy with me and I backed away because I couldn't trust her. I blocked her on social media and told her the craziness she was spewing there was too much for me. She acknowledged her lack of abstinence was killing her and that she was powerless to stop. I guess suicide seemed to her the only way out.

I share these stories so the lesson of them is not lost. Addiction is a powerful killer of a disease.

I tried to commit suicide in my early 20's. It was one of two times in my life since 6th grade I didn't have a job. I was studying in Mexico. Take away my drugs and I'm a live nerve.

My disease is all about escaping. Let me escape the pain of my situation, my fears, my obsessions and inadequacy. Suicide is the ultimate escape.

My recovery is all about finding the courage to face the difficult and uncomfortable stuff life throws at me. And when I stick around and don't try to escape, I get amazing rewards.

Being where I am   May 19

When I was first in recovery, I heard addicts want to be anywhere else, doing anything else, with anyone else, at all times. We're restless, irritable and discontented.

Most 12-Step meetings begin with a moment of silence. My first sponsor said she used the moment to say to herself "I'm exactly where I'm supposed to be." I still say that same thing. It is calming to my often-racing mind. It works on two levels: I'm physically supposed to be at that meeting right then and also my life is not worse than it is supposed to be, whether financially, spiritually, emotionally, relationship-wise, health-wise, weight-wise, recovery-wise, job-wise.

Recovery right-sizes me.

Adrenaline   May 20

We do not get 'wound up,' so we do not have to unwind. – The Workaholics Anonymous Book of Recovery, *2nd Edition, p. 30.*

For so many years, I got wound up every day at work, and then I needed to unwind in the evening. I skipped lunch because the pressure was so intense I could tell myself I didn't have the time to eat. My adrenaline kept me going so I didn't even get hungry. Until I got home after work and crashed. I would be starving, so I would eat readily available junk food, and too much of it.

Today, I keep an eye on my perceived pressure and take steps to counteract the pressure instead of getting wound up. I eat lunch before I'm hungry and I plan my dinner by mid-day, so there's less chance of a compulsive binge. My adrenaline level stays even all day, and there's no sharp drop off when I turn off my computer so my emotional state is not as prone to highs and lows.

Rollercoasters   May 21

When I was a kid, I loved rollercoasters. What a rush. However, from age twenty-five to forty, I refused to go on rollercoasters because I couldn't stand the feeling of being out of control. This was not conducive to raising kids who loved rollercoasters. My husband had to wait in a lot of long lines at amusement parks.

When I got into recovery, I came to see rollercoasters as a form of Step 3 surrender. I would let go of my need to control the situation, trust God would get me safely back to land again, and I would be fine. Sometimes I said the third step prayer to myself as the coaster made the steep trip up to the top. I came to love rollercoasters again, another unexpected gift of recovery.

Workaholic Culture   May 22

Recently, my hard-working son graduated from a prestigious university. Anna Quindlen, a Pulitzer Prize winning journalist, gave the commencement address. Some of her advice to these ambitious students could have been right out of a Workaholics Anonymous meeting:

You are the people who make the checklists, who come up with plans, who are invested always in the right answer. ...The checklist should be honored mostly in the breach. The plans are a tiny box that, followed slavishly, will smother you.

...[I]f you as a group ditch what has somehow become the 80-hour work week and return us to a sane investment in our personal and professional lives, you will have done better than us.

And she talked about fear. That we can't let fear stop us from doing the right thing, even if that looks like failure or weakness. Fear fueled so much of my workaholism. And standing up and doing the next right thing despite the fear has been such a signpost of my recovery and success against this disease.

Our culture of workaholism is everywhere around us. It's so exciting for me to see references in mainstream culture encouraging our best and brightest not to buy into it.

Integrity   May 23

Text to sponsor: "I hope you are having a good day. I got a bootleg copy of "Hamilton the Musical" today. I *really* want to watch it. *Really*. I'm conflicted about the copyright infringement. I won't get to see the original cast perform "Hamilton." I want to set a good example for my kids and others. I discuss "Hamilton" with everyone who will listen, and I'm sure if I have seen this bootleg, it will come up. They will ask me to send a link. I don't like not being in integrity about creative rights. Arrrrgh. Today, I commit to not watching it."

Although this was a difficult decision, I am proud of myself. My sponsor said, "Having principles can be uncomfortable and inconvenient, can't it? If it weren't, everyone would have them."

Doing the right next thing comes in so many forms. I'm sure many people would not have a moral dilemma over this. I'm sure other people struggle with issues that I don't give a second thought to. What matters is I honor my moral code. When I do, I build my self-esteem. My addict feeds off low self-esteem. If I take the opportunities presented to increase my self-esteem, I gain a little insurance against the next slip.

Control and Surrender   May 24

Anna, one of my program friends, committed suicide recently. On Saturday following her death, there was some ambiguity over who had agreed to chair Anna's Wednesday home group. It was either me or another member, June. I contacted June and asked how strongly she felt about chairing and told her I would like to do it. She didn't seem inclined to give it up, so I went along with her decision. We discussed taking a group conscience to change the format to a memorial service just for one night.

Then I began to second guess my acquiescence and wondered if I was taking the easy way out, when I should be chairing the meeting. I worried June wouldn't handle it right and Anna's many friends and former sponsees would be further traumatized. I started obsessing about it. So, I called my sponsor. She gave me permission to stand down. She said my concern for everyone's well-being was misplaced. I should just take each day as it comes and try to be available to whatever God had in mind for me. My obsession abated and I was again at peace. I put together a lovely eulogy for Anna and I arranged for a group dinner before the meeting on Wednesday.

Then, amazingly, I got a call from June late Tuesday night, asking if I could chair the meeting for her the next evening. Of course, I agreed. Someone brought a candle and we dimmed the fluorescent lights. Anna's roommate spoke first, giving some details surrounding the suicide. One member donated her three-minute share time for a meditation. And everyone shared their experiences of Anna. It was beautiful and cathartic. I felt I had surrendered to God's will and everything worked out as God intended.

Obsession   May 25

I had lots of obsession over the weekend concerning a work project. Not a substantive law matter, but rather a technical question of how to file certain documents online. I was afraid of being found out as a fraud. I was afraid I would look bad in front of one of my partners. I kept reminding myself to put off thinking about it until 9am on Monday. I meditated and asked God what His will was for me. Maybe God's will is for me is to fail and get some humility. I spoke to a sponsee about it. I brought it up at a WA meeting. Maybe I can ask for help from someone with experience? I try not to pester people with work emails on the weekend, but on Sunday night, I reached out to my paralegal and to one of my partners. I was hoping they wouldn't be on email on Sunday night, but rather would see it first thing on Monday. As it turned out, my paralegal had just the experience I was lacking. I now have hope.

As a result of this difficult weekend of obsession, I wrote down some ideas so next time, I can turn to the solution sooner.
Options when I'm stuck in obsession:
1. Talk to someone about it.
2. Pray.
3. Write about it.
4. Talk about it at a meeting.
5. Delegate.
6. Ask for help—do I know someone with relevant experience?

7. Surrender—what is God's will?
8. Consider what's the worst that can happen; it's usually something I can accept.
9. Have I ever had a similar situation and what was the resolution? How long did it take? It's usually resolved within a week, maybe even a day.
10. Call my sponsor.
11. Take suggestions.
12. Think about how I can be of service to someone.
13. Relax and take it easy.

Not all the suggestions are relevant for every obsession, but if I contemplate a whole host of possibilities, one of them might be the right one for the job.

The best bridge between despair and hope is a good night's rest. – overheard at a WA meeting

Serenity in a Storm   May 26

The last few months have been busy at work. Every time I thought about work, I felt pressure I wasn't getting it all done in time. I was sure something was going to fall through the cracks and come back to bite me.

Then, lately, I caught up many of my longer-term projects so it feels more under control. I have been less anxious the last several days. I wish I didn't need "being in control" to have peace. The goal is to be secure even when there's a lot going on. The problem is I make productivity and control my higher power. My real Higher Power doesn't care if I've caught up all my work projects. My real Higher Power loves me even when I'm not in control.

Wouldn't it be great to feel serene even in the midst of a storm?

Mystery of WA   May 27

At the beginning of my WA recovery, I was skeptical as to whether WA could make sense of my workaholism. When I went to the office, it was like going to a buffet without a food plan. I would taste a little of this and that and want more of that one. Work and personal tasks lined up, calling out to me. There was no rhyme or reason about what was most important or how long things would take. It was a binge waiting to happen.

Luckily, I could look back on my experience in Overeaters Anonymous and see I had been equally mystified about how OA could help me with my food. I'd seen the magic in OA. Was it such a stretch to have that same sanity I now have in my relationship with food appear in my relationship with time and activities? The beginning of my OA journey was mysterious, so I just had to trust more would be revealed in my WA journey.

Now that I've been in WA a number of years, I can see the tools of the program subtly worked their magic on me, just the same as happened with food. I have clarity and priorities and more honest assessments of "How important is it?"

I have come to believe the power of WA can restore my life to sanity.

Punctuality   May 28

You know those people who are always running late? Well, that's not me. I have the opposite problem. I'm punctual to a fault. I always thought this was a virtue, until I saw how it affected my relationships with my family when I tried to control them around being early.

My Higher Power had this to say: "It is pleasant not to rush. However, it is selfish of you only to consider your need for emotional security when you demand the whole family to leave extra early so you're on time."

Today, I try to act as if I'm sane about arrival times and keep my anxiety to myself. I try to calm my anxiety by repeating this affirmation (to myself): "It is okay if I'm late sometimes."

Service Overload   May 29

At one of my 12-Step meetings, I was frustrated because I seemed to be the only one doing service. I chaired the meeting and acted as treasurer and literature person. I was sponsoring a bunch of women in the meeting. I repeatedly let the meeting know we needed people to sign up for these various duties. No one had as much time in the program as I did. I went to my sponsor and said I think I had to stop going to the meeting, because I was feeling so resentful.

My sponsor had other ideas. She said I needed to keep going to the meeting, but to stop doing the various duties. She said we should let the 7th Tradition accumulate in the meeting box until someone stepped up. Instead of having someone sign up to chair for a month, ask at the end of the meeting if anyone would commit to chair the following week. If no one volunteered, let it go to the next week and ask at the beginning of the meeting if anyone would agree to chair that night. She said to leave the literature in the box, until someone stepped up and put it out. I objected because what would happen to the newcomer who walked in and didn't find any literature? I wanted the newcomers to have the same great experience I did walking into my first meeting. She said the newcomer would have a better experience at the meeting if I was present and sober, rather than absent and resentful.

So, I took her suggestion. I kept showing up and exercised self-restraint about doing duties that rightfully belonged to others in the meeting. Eventually, people stepped up. Nature abhors a vacuum. Today, that meeting is thriving and I do only my fair share of service in it.

Sober service is giving from my overflow. – overheard at a WA meeting

I am Loveable and Capable   May 30

When I was twelve, my school participated in a program in which we made these paper signs we wore on the front of our shirts which said "IALAC." This stood for "I am loveable and capable." It was my first introduction to affirmations. I remember thinking at the time, and at various times over the years, "I believe I'm capable, but I don't for one second believe I am loveable." So, I worked that capable stuff for all it was worth.

Isn't it ironic that a program intended to help kids with self-esteem seems to have completely back-fired in my case?

Relationship with a Group   May 31

Over and over in my life, I desperately wanted various groups to accept me, and couldn't figure out the secret. In grade school, it was the cool kids. In college, the sorority. In my professional life, my peers. Then later I got into recovery and wanted people in my 12-Step meetings to accept me. People have a strange way of noticing I'm only in it for myself. They could tell I didn't care about them, that I only wanted their love and not vice versa. So, when I showed up to events of each group, I felt awkward and conspicuous in my failure to fit in. What I had failed to do all along was to form relationships with the individuals that make up the group.

I had an opportunity to practice this in one of my meetings. I started acting "as if" I cared about the members. I answered my phone when people made outreach calls. I showed up to be of service. I attended the business meetings. I went out for fellowship to get to know what was going on with these people beyond what they shared in meetings. Eventually, I acted my way into right thinking with my behavior, and came to love them.

Today, I talk to many of the members throughout the week, or exchange texts with them, so I know what is going on in their lives and can ask them about it. When I show up at that meeting today, I feel at home and welcome. If I connect with the individuals, the group takes care of itself.

Meditation Retreat vs Work Conference   June 1

Every May, my profession holds a huge conference—a gathering of 10,000 professionals from around the world. I usually go and spend morning to night in meetings. It has long been a sponsor-approved exception to my usual work week of 25 hours.

This year, I had the opportunity to attend a retreat with a teacher important to my meditation practice. While it didn't conflict exactly with the work conference, it was too close for comfort. (Before recovery, I would have gone to both.) So, taking a deep breath, I opted for the meditation retreat. As the time got closer for the work conference and the emails were flying about people being out of town and asking me for meetings, I was so happy with my decision. I skipped all that stress this year. I didn't feel left out or irrelevant. My practice hasn't fallen apart yet. I even put up an out-of-office message on my email, so I wouldn't feel pressure to check my email while on retreat.

And the meditation retreat was pretty much the exact opposite of the work conference.

Acceptance and Step 2   June 2

Step 2 talks about restoring me to sanity. The tool of Acceptance helps me stop fighting reality, which is totally insane. God has control over outcomes, I do not. The sooner I accept situations in my life which are "unacceptable" to me, the sooner I find resolution. As long as I'm fighting acceptance, I'm blocked to answers. Insanity continues.

When I struggle with accepting something in my life, I can turn to these wise words in the *AA Big Book*:

Acceptance is the answer to ALL of my problems today. When I am disturbed, it is because I find some person, place, thing or situation- some fact of my life- unacceptable to me, and I can find no serenity until I accept that person, place, thing, or situation as being exactly the way it is supposed to be at this moment. Nothing, absolutely nothing, happens in God's world by mistake. Until I could accept my alcoholism, I could not stay sober; unless I accept my life completely on life's terms, I cannot be happy. I need to concentrate not so much on what needs to be changed in the world as on what needs to be changed in me and in my attitudes. - Page 417, Alcoholics Anonymous

Meditation June 3

Just because I know meditation is good for me doesn't mean I always do it. When there is structure to my day and I'm clear when meditation fits in, then it happens. For instance, if I had to get up and take the kids to school and then go to the office, I would plan to get up early enough to have my quiet time. But on those days when I didn't take the kids to school and I could go into the office really early to start getting things done, well, then, meditation was the first thing I didn't do. Sometimes I would remember after I got to the office, and I would close my door and sit on the office floor to meditate.

These days, I work from home, and I don't take the kids to school anymore. This was challenging at first. After walking the dogs, I could go up the stairs and take a right into my office, or a left to my bedroom to meditate. As I had just started my own business, I was eager to get to work and make a success of it. But I knew how important meditation was to my recovery. Finally, I made a commitment to one of my sponsees: I would have to tell her if I ever miss my prayer and meditation time. Well, that straightened me out. I get right on it. The only time I miss my quiet time today is sometimes when I'm travelling, out of my routine, I simply forget and get caught up in everything else. But then I tell on myself to my sponsee.

Fun June 4

One of my character defects is taking myself and life too seriously. I can work and work all day on my client's projects and on my personal to-do list, but it never occurs to me to just take an hour and blow off doing something frivolous and non-productive. I fear I would not be satisfied later in the day because I could have gotten more stuff done.

When I was working on my 6th step, my sponsor suggested I ask God for his input about this. Here is what I heard: "When your son is working so hard on school work he doesn't seem to ever have fun and relax, you feel bad. That's how I feel when you refuse to take a break. I didn't put you there for a life of drudgery. I'm so happy for you when you take time away from being productive and just enjoy the many gifts I gave you."

In the face of all of my inner voices to the contrary, I tell myself this affirmation: "Fun is valuable." Maybe someday I'll believe it.

Multitasking

A lot has been said and written about multitasking. Some claim proficiency proudly. I used to try to multitask. I have found it is insane, particularly while driving. I used to check my email and text while driving. Look up a phone number and try to dial while driving. My brain gets stressed, overstimulated and adrenalized when I'm trying to accomplish multiple goals at the same time. This comes from my belief there's not enough time and everything is urgent. I need to use drive time to check more things off my list.

Today, I try to focus on one goal at a time. (I'm not perfect at it, and I make exceptions, such as talking on the phone and driving, talking on the phone and walking, talking on the phone when preparing food that doesn't require attention to a recipe. I like to talk on the phone a lot.) Doing one thing at a time allows my brain to function optimally to do the one job correctly, and also allows an infusion of intuition from my Higher Power into the process, to ensure I make decisions consistent with God's will.

Wasting Time
June 6

Lately I've been debating whether to get my hair cut really short. Most of my adult life I have had long hair. One of the advantages of long hair has been I virtually never need to spend time on haircuts. I realized when I was weighing the pros and cons, the deciding factor seemed to be my frustration and fear with wasting time having to get it trimmed every 6-8 weeks. So, in discussing this with my Higher Power, I came to believe God wants me to cut my hair, at least for now, and each time I get a trim, I shall make it an act of connection with my Higher Power.

Jealousy: Compare and Despair
June 7

Jealousy is so painful and lacking in any redemptive quality. There will always be people who have more than me. I am lucky I haven't struggled a lot with jealousy in my life. But one time I found it debilitating.

When I worked at a large law firm, I went through a period in which I compared myself to my work colleagues and found myself envious of their success, clients, sense of humor, articulateness, brilliance, strategic thinking, creativity, and how they seemed to ask for and get what they wanted. This was a deep cavern into which I fell. I felt that others looked at me and made the same comparison. They saw how I came up short. Perhaps my firm would fire me at any moment. It was so ugly.

I did a resentment inventory about my colleagues and got into honesty about how hard they had worked and how much they had sacrificed to build the practices they had. I began praying for help with this jealousy every morning. I asked God to help me focus on how I can be useful to my colleagues, clients and firm, instead of looking out for what's in it for me. That small change in attitude did great wonders. The jealousy went away and I've never suffered from it again.

Visioning   June 8

Once a month my WA meeting does a visioning exercise taken from <u>How to Get Out of Debt, Stay Out of Debt and Live Prosperously</u> by Jerrold Mundis (pp. 226-29). We read the following:
If I could be, do and have everything I want:
- *Describe the ideal for you*
- *Let go of your inhibitions, all sense of restriction and limitation*
- *Unleash your wishes and desires, and let them run free*
- *Describe what you would truly want, not what you think you ought to want*
- *Speak in the present tense as if you are already there*
- *Your subconscious already knows what you want. You have just been hiding it from yourself.*
-

We each write for ten minutes what our vision for our lives looks like, and we can share our vision if we want.

Here is my most recent vision for myself: I don't suffer from anxiety, and I trust my Higher Power with everything. I don't worry and I am carefree. I have an easy-going attitude and I don't micromanage myself, anyone or anything in my life.

Bathroom Breaks   June 9

I can't tell you how many times I have delayed going to the bathroom so I could get one more thing done at my desk. I can't imagine telling my staff "No, you can't go to the bathroom until you finish this task" and then give them another one to do. I would never treat other people that way. But that's how I treated myself.

When I got into recovery from workaholism, one of my bottom lines was to go to the bathroom *as soon as I felt* the *urge*. I am much better about this now. It seems like such a little thing, but it means a lot in terms of self-care and having respect for myself.

Ego   June 10

I meant to sit down and meditate or nap from 4-4:30 today but picked up my phone instead to check my email, which led me to returning calls, which led to me talking to a reporter. He wanted to know my opinion as to whether a certain practice constituted copyright infringement. I was flattered and vociferously voiced my opinion, acting as though there was no room for argument and hoping he quoted me in his article. As soon as I got off the call, I realized my opinion could be the opposite of a position being taken by my law firm in a client case and now I might be quoted. That could be awkward for the client and my firm.

If I had been trying to do God's will, I would have listened to the voice telling me to put my phone down and take a break. Instead, I went crashing on, with my ego running the show. First, my ego was in charge when I was hoping for recognition and admiration by being quoted. Second, my ego was in fear, not because my quote would hurt my firm or our client, but because it could reflect badly on me. I can be so self-centered, particularly around work image issues.

I realize awareness is the first step in me changing my workaholic behavior. I now have more awareness about my character defect that seeks glory. Hopefully, the next time I speak to a reporter I can pause and reflect on other considerations that might temper my ego's enthusiasm.

Talking about Work   June 11

For most of my life, I have had far more energy around work than other people do. I would obsess and talk about it incessantly. I wore out my husband and sisters with constant discussion of my work and complaints about my work colleagues. "Can you believe what so-and-so did now?" I brought endless judgement, drama and gossip. Other people are not as fascinated with my work as I am. It makes me a bore.

106

Since I've been in recovery from workaholism, I carefully select how much I discuss work with others in my life, so I keep perspective and not use work talk like a junkie. I try to avoid gossiping, both on the work front and in life. This forces me to develop interests in other aspects of life, so I can talk about other subjects.

Withdrawal   June 12

When I first joined Workaholics Anonymous and began working with a sponsor, she encouraged me to start slowing down. She told me to take breaks to just do nothing. She suggested I stop multitasking—to walk my dog or get my nails done without being on my phone. My sponsor said if I'm going to eat my lunch at my desk at least not work at the same time. She encouraged me to play with my kids.

In those early weeks and months, I took her suggestions and often felt like crawling out of my skin. One night, I had a panic attack. Night after night, I had trouble sleeping. I felt guilty taking a nap in the middle of the day when I could be working. My sponsor told me I wasn't slacking, but rather I was beginning to work at a normal pace. I can now see this was my withdrawal from workaholism. Eventually, the discomfort waned. I began to appreciate the benefits of rest and how taking breaks fostered creative intuition to help me solve problems.

Identity = Profession   June 13

For as long as I can remember, I identified myself based on what I did. I was a student, a legal secretary, a paralegal, law student, a lawyer, a law partner, a law professor or a board member. I wrapped up my self-worth in whatever position I occupied professionally. My value was equal to my work accomplishments. If I lost my job and were no longer a lawyer, I feared I would not be important or respected.

Today, I try to be ok with valuing myself for just being me and knowing even if I weren't a lawyer or a partner at a law firm, I will still be loved and accepted by God and others. For instance, by limiting the time I work, the time I spend obsessing about work, choosing other priorities instead of work from time to time, taking vacations, etc., all of these help provide me a more well-rounded life, instead of one dominated by work, so I have other interests and roles for me to identify with. My efforts in my work addiction program are all chipping away at my screwed-up identification.

Superiority/Inferiority   June 14

In my disease, I vacillate between feeling like I'm better than everybody else, or I'm less than everybody else. Thinking I'm superior to others is a way to make me feel good about myself. Dwelling on others' shortcomings means I'm not facing my own. On the other hand, my disease also can get stuck comparing myself unfavorably to others, wishing I had what they had, coming up short.

Both situations feel yucky. Although I may momentarily enjoy the self-satisfaction of superiority, if I indulge in feeling "better than," inevitably the "worse than" situation will rear its ugly head.

Sobriety has a way of moderating this teeter-totter. Sobriety leads me to truth, and when I honestly look at my circumstances, I can see that I have some gifts and other people have different gifts. Sobriety itself is a gift, and there's no reason why I should be enjoying it, while others continue to suffer from work addiction. I'm no more deserving than others.

It is not useful for me to spend time feeling either superior or inferior to others. It is useful for me to appreciate what I have and do what I can to help those less fortunate than I am. Sobriety brings with it humility to be in the middle and to be ok with that.

Mistakes   June 15

I used to think making mistakes was unacceptable. It indicated a fundamental weakness or stupidity. If I made the mistake myself, I suffered shame. If my staff made a mistake, I was livid, yelling and shaming them because I will look bad in front of the client, who will think I'm an idiot.

I now appreciate a different way to look at mistakes. First, when I make a mistake, I try to forgive myself. Thinking I'm immune from mistakes is my ego talking: I should be better than everyone else. Everyone else gets to learn and experiment, but I am an extraordinary human who skips all that and knows better without having been taught.

Second, if someone who works for me makes a mistake, today I'm quick to ignore it and move into triage mode—how can we fix it and prevent it from happening again? I tell my staff my expectation is they should be making mistakes at least 5% of the time. If not, it means they are in perfectionism, checking and rechecking their work. That is not efficient and the clients can't afford to be paying extra by the hour to have perfection.

Using Program Tools   June 16

I had delegated a project to one of my associates, Tom, and was angry at him today about how messed up it was. I've spoken with him about this kind of problem before. Even if the problem is with his secretary, he should have explained how he planned to resolve it instead of ignoring it and leaving it for me to fix.

The good news is I honored one of my bottom lines and didn't yell at him in email or otherwise. I reminded myself I'm never happy when I say mean things in email and I need to wait until I can speak with him to hear his explanation. I simply asked him to call me when he's free.

I also honored another bottom line by not gossiping about him to another colleague. I soothed myself in a mini-inventory by honestly facing realities—perhaps Tom doesn't have the skill or training to do this kind of work yet.

I called my sponsor. She reminded me I have skills Tom doesn't. He probably has skills I don't have. She recommended I ask Tom, "What's going on?" I should try to get him to be present to the problem. What can I say to him so he can hear me? My disease resists this: I don't want to take the time and I don't think I should be bothered with this training. She suggested I explain to Tom why this part of the project is important. Show him how his handling is causing me a problem. Remind him we've talked about this before and it still isn't fixed. Tell him I'd like to brainstorm with him the problem and what the solution might be.

I find when I use program tools such as bottom lines, sponsors and taking suggestions, my toolkit isn't limited to the inadequate few I had when I came into WA. I can handle anger with dignity. I can get results that solve problems.

Workaholic Culture   June 17

One of my goals in recovery from workaholism is to keep my work within the 9-5 work day. Sometimes that isn't possible because I work with people in other time zones but, for the most part, I can do it.

One way I perpetuated a workaholic culture was to send work emails or leave voicemails outside normal business hours. This encouraged other people to be checking and responding to emails and vmails on their personal time. It sent the signal I was available to work evenings and weekends. I have tried to stop doing this. Even if I need to work on a project outside normal work hours, I can hold off sending it until first thing the next business day. This is hard for me because I'm a people pleaser. I want to impress clients and my partners with my industriousness and responsiveness.

I now encourage my staff to practice restraint with each other with respect to sending emails outside work hours. Again, I make exceptions for urgent work, but this is such a small percentage of the total work flow everyone can understand the difference, and we can all enjoy a good weekend.

Intensity   June 18

Here's a journal entry from the days when I was still commuting to an office downtown to work:

"Today presented a zoo of emergencies at the office. I spent the whole day on adrenalin going from one fire to another. I couldn't stop checking and responding to my email for a good hour after I got home. Originally, my plan was to work from home tomorrow. Had a battle with myself about whether to go into the office anyway. Directly after work, I was *convinced* that I needed to be there, even though I knew tonight would be a late night out. I even drafted an email to my sponsor explaining/rationalizing my change of plan, only to erase it all.

Now I've calmed down a little and recommitted to working from home tomorrow. One of the tools in my toolkit is, when faced with one intense and one less intense option, to choose the less intense route. It makes my life so much easier."

The soul does not grow by *addition* but by *subtraction*.
– Meister Eckhart

Sponsee Overload   June 19

Some of my 12-Step fellowships say "never say no to service." This is a quandary for a work addict. There's no end to the amount of service one can do, in and outside the rooms. At one point, I had 10 sponsees actively working the steps, which meant I had at least 10 hours of meetings with them a week, not including ad hoc calls. It began to impinge on my professional work and my family. My life had become unmanageable. So, I asked my sponsor for suggestions. She suggested that I bring it up at 12-Step meetings and see if others had found solutions.

When I did that, one suggestion was to gather the sponsees together if they were at a similar place in their stepwork and meet with them as a group. I hated this idea. My sponsor gave me one-on-one attention. I didn't want to deprive any of my sponsees of that experience. But, I took the suggestion.

My sponsees weren't thrilled with it initially, but once we began meeting, they got to know one another. They started getting together with each other before and after our meetings for fellowship, calling one another for support in between meetings, and generally enjoying the benefits of having sister sponsees. Never in my wildest dreams would I have imagined this situation benefitting my sponsees. It goes to show me how once again I can be wrong about something I've never tried, and yet be certain I'm right.

Pressure   June 20

We do not yield to pressure from others or attempt to pressure others. – The Workaholics Anonymous Book of Recovery, 2nd Edition, p. 30.

Recently, I've had interest from other lawyers about joining my law firm. One of the owners, Sarah, mentioned she would be in Chicago in two weeks, and if I wanted to set up meetings with the candidates, she would be happy to meet with them. We like to have candidates talk to five or six partners as part of the interview process. On Monday before Sarah was to meet with the recruits, another owner, Steve, told me all of the partner interviews should be completed before Sarah meets with the candidates, so she could make offers during her meetings with them. That made me uncomfortable because I didn't have control over when my partners and the candidates could make time in their busy schedules to meet. So, I told Steve and Sarah, "That was not my understanding when I set up Sarah's meetings. If that is important, then we should cancel Sarah's meetings with the recruits and have her meet with them later." Sarah immediately stepped in and agreed to meet with the candidates regardless of where they were in the process. I felt good I stood up for myself and diffused the unnecessary pressure Steve was creating. This is new behavior for me, particularly with an authority figure.

Quitting Jobs   June 21

I have quit several jobs because I let my ego call the shots. Once, my supervisor wrote me up for something I thought was unfair, and another time my management passed me over for a promotion. Both times, I was humiliated. As a workaholic, my drug of choice is the admiration and affirmation I get from work. In both situations, I got the opposite of my drug, so I quit.

My reaction was out of proportion to the harm done. I had no thought for my best interest long term. I just wanted to escape from the pain and the people who knew of my humiliation as quickly as possible. Ironically, they probably didn't notice the original slight to me, but they likely lost respect for me for how I handled it.

Today, I hope I would be more thoughtful and less reactive about running away from a difficult situation. Hopefully, I would see my pride for what it is—a barrier to my improvement.

Rest   June 22

My bottom lines call for me to not check my work email on the weekends. I've been sticking to that. I feel my brain is cycling down from constant input. It is unstimulated for long stretches of time. I now believe this is a rejuvenating state to be in periodically. My brain is not always being called on to make connections and solve problems. Sometimes it gets to take a rest. This will ultimately allow deeper thoughts, intuition and improved prioritization.

Fun   June 23

The meeting I attended when I first came into WA followed a typical WA meeting format for three weeks of every month. But on the

4th meeting, we played gin rummy. How I hated those weeks. I needed the information I was getting from the regular meetings. I needed the readings. I needed to identify with other members' shares. I couldn't believe they were wasting everybody's time with a game. When a newcomer showed up for his or her first WA meeting on game day, I was mortified and felt certain they would never return.

I see now the game days served a vital purpose. I can be workaholic even in my working a WA program. I don't allow time for fun and frivolity. I always have to be on task. The game days forced me to do what I couldn't do for myself and showed me how desperately I needed to not take myself so seriously.

Telecommuting   June 24

At the beginning of my WA journey, I worked part-time at a huge law firm in downtown Chicago. I was in the office 9-3 Monday-Friday. About one month after I began working the steps with a sponsor in WA, it occurred to me, when I had given myself a moment without outside stimulus, I could work from home one day a week. I told myself, "It would be ok."

Working from home turned out to be amazing. I was more productive because I didn't have to get dressed and commute to the office. I was also more relaxed.

A year later, I gave myself permission to start telecommuting a second day each week. Again, I experienced nothing but positives from this change; no one at work cared I wasn't putting in as much face time. In fact, some days at the office I wouldn't see a single person I worked with because so much of my work was with people in other states or countries, so we relied on phone and email to conduct business.

Finally, after being in WA for six years, I left that job and joined a virtual law firm which allowed me to work exclusively from home. I have now been working virtually for 3 years and I have never looked back. It is the best of all possible worlds for me. I know some people don't care to work from home because they get distracted by home chores or they prefer the structure or collegiality of working at an office. I'm not troubled by those issues. Of course, it probably helps in this case I'm a workaholic and can't wait to be back at my desk...

Media Checking   June 25

One of the compulsive behaviors I still struggle with is checking my phone obsessively at every lull in the day, every break in the action. I want a hit from whatever new email, text or posting might be there to give me something new to read, do or react to. As an activity addict, I can't stand to be quiet, without distraction or stimulation.

When I'm in a spiritually connected place, I can notice the urge to check my phone or computer and sit with it, without acting. This can be excruciating, like having an itch and not scratching. What if someone is trying to reach me?

The more I practice, the better I get at being ok with no new stimulation. I find this to be particularly rewarding when I'm tired. I tell myself it's time to take a break from input and just rest. I'm so grateful after my rest I gave myself that gift.

10th Step   June 26

The 10th step says "*Continued to take personal inventory and when we were wrong, promptly admitted it.*" Someone pointed out this step says "when" I am wrong. That is different from "if." Use of the word "when" means it is inevitable I will be wrong. That I'm expected to be wrong. That being wrong is part of the human condition. What a relief to know being wrong is ok. Of course, I don't go out of my way to make mistakes but, because I'm human, it is not always obvious what the right next thing is, so sometimes I'm going to take wrong turns. And then I can admit it and set things right. I can go through life with a lighter attitude and shed the weight and pressure of worrying about making the right choice or being perfect.

A daily 10th step inventory is like taking out the garbage. If you don't do it, it's gonna get stinky in here. – overheard at a WA meeting

Adrenalizing   June 27

The WA literature says adrenalizing is creating pressure, suspense and chaos. I adrenalize by time-stuffing, multitasking, not planning ahead, over-committing and hurrying. I work with a sense of urgency—the fear I won't get everything done in time—and there's a tightness between my shoulders. By creating this sense of urgency, I get a hit from the rush of adrenaline. I carry a pharmacy complete with my drug of choice in my own body. It only works if I believe the lie my disease tells me that the urgency is real.

I had never heard of WA when a friend from another 12-Step program called me to say she was feeling pressure from her workload, so she thought she would make a call to help her ease the pressure. This sounded insane. If you feel pressure because you have too much work to do, do the work and the pressure will go away. You don't have time for calls!

This was the wakeup call that got me to my first WA meeting.

Today I understand the pressure and urgency I feel is my disease and it is not inevitable. This was totally news to me. I thought the work caused the urgency, but actually, it is something I do to myself. When I feel urgency, the next right thing to do is get up from my desk, go to the bathroom, get a cup of coffee, or call someone. I can use any number of tools, such as prioritizing, under-scheduling, relaxing, taking a time out or doing some honest self-talk about the nature of the tasks in front of me, with an emphasis on just how unimportant they are in the big scheme of things or how they are not urgent and can wait.

Productivity and Value   June 28

One of my character defects is thinking being productive defines my value. Every day I make a to-do list of what I need or want to accomplish that day. When I'm in my disease, my self-worth at the end of the day is dependent on whether I achieved the goals I set out for myself. When I'm in recovery, I can be ok with myself if I fell short of my goals. Maybe circumstances shifted and I had to rearrange priorities. Maybe I needed a nap more than anything.

My Higher Power tells me: "It doesn't all need to get done today. Be still and know that I am God."

An affirmation I can use to help remind me: "I have value even if I'm not being productive. It is ok to just "be" some of the day."

Eating   June 29

In the worst of my workaholism, I would skip or delay meals because I wanted to get the project *du jour* done, and often I identified just one more task, and another, until it was time to go home for the night. My adrenaline flooded my body from the stress of the work, which diminished my appetite. Then I crashed after the adrenaline stopped pumping and I binged on food in the evening because I starved myself all day. The food was not healthy because I didn't have the patience or foresight to grocery shop and cook, so I just ate whatever was expedient, which was often pizza.

As part of my recovery, I eat according to a food plan, at specific times of the day. I don't have to be rigid, but it is important to know what I'm eating in advance, and to plan healthy options. Today, I eat healthily every day and it is a vital part of my overall recovery from workaholism.

Matching Energy   June 30

One of the themes on my inventory was my resentment of people who had been wonderful mentors and friends to me at my job, but when I stopped working with them, they no longer had any use for me. I thought my relationships with these mentors was much more important and that we would continue in each others' lives even if I wasn't working with them. It made me sad they didn't return my affection or my calls. I felt used.

My sponsor helped me move toward acceptance by explaining I don't get to pick who I love in this life. Not everyone is going to be as attracted to me as I am to them. It is my job to love those who show up in my life. And for those who have less energy for me than I have for them, it is appropriate for me to simply match their energy, not stalk them. I don't need to cut them off altogether, but if they want to see me for lunch once a year, then I should go to lunch with them once a year. And I should let them do the inviting to lunch every other year. If lunch stops happening, it's time for me to spend my energy elsewhere.

I was able to forgive those mentors, and not be hurt because their lives were full enough without me. I could accept graciously what they had to offer.

"Get Lost" Meditation July 1

One meditation technique I prefer is called "Get Lost." Like most people, when I sit down to meditate, I have no problem getting lost and falling down a rabbit hole of thought or emotion. I struggle to stay on task and aware.

With the "Get Lost" meditation, I sit with a pen and paper, or some other way of counting, and I tell myself to go ahead and get lost. Every time I notice that I've forgotten to be aware of where and when I am, I make a hash mark. The more hash marks at the end of my meditation, the better. This way, I'm rewarded for getting lost, but also for coming back to awareness. Counterintuitively, I stay more aware during this kind of meditation than traditional meditation—it is like my thoughts become shy when summoned. Or else my mind is just a brat.

Teachers July 2

When I was in high school, I had an Honors Spanish teacher—Sr. Mendoza—with whom I constantly butted heads. It always meant a lot to me that my teachers liked me, and this one didn't. I was ok only when I received A's and I was quite certain this teacher would go out of his way to give me bad grades. I complained about my teacher to the administration. My Dean and the regular Spanish teacher figured out a way for me to go to the regular Spanish class and simply do extra work in order to qualify my work as Honors. Sr. Mendoza was an average teacher, but since he didn't worship the ground I walked on, I made life so difficult in his room they found another place for me.

When I inventoried this resentment, I found that Sr. Mendoza threatened my emotional security because I was secure only when people held me in high esteem, particularly people who had authority over me. My ambition also was in jeopardy because I wanted great grades.

I see now how selfishly I behaved. I wanted my way, which was to get out of Sr. Mendoza's class, and still get Honors credit. The only thing I cared about was my grades. I gossiped about Sr. Mendoza to whoever would listen, and I badmouthed him to the administration. I was also being fearful—I thought I needed Sr. Mendoza's approval to be ok. I was afraid this teacher who didn't like me would give me a bad grade. And I was dishonest—in reality, my grade from one teacher didn't matter, and I would be ok if I stayed connected to God.

Once I worked through this situation in my step work, I realized I needed to make amends both to Sr. Mendoza and to the administration at my high school, which I did.

Broccoli tasks   July 3

Sometimes I get resentful about the tasks I'm supposed to do. Especially paperwork, such as filling out forms to register my kids for summer camp, or taking care of medical tests and procedures, or writing an inventory about someone who upset me. I convince myself no one else has to do these chores, I get into self-pity and I procrastinate.

My sponsor once told me that everyone has tasks in their life that are broccoli. Broccoli and other vegetables are not the sexiest and most attractive of foods. Yet if I eat my broccoli, I get lots of benefits from a health perspective. If I just do the broccoli tasks, my life is so much better. I don't miss deadlines which would complicate my life immeasurably. Health issues aren't exacerbated which could make my life unmanageable. "A stitch in time saves nine." While it might sound like a workaholic proverb, admonishing me to always be on top of everything, the end goal of the proverb is less work, not more.

Control   July 4

One of my character defects is needing things to be "under control" for me to relax. I hate leaving a project in the middle. For me, closure is often my disease. I don't think I'll be ok if something is left unfinished, ambiguous, not figured out. I'm uncomfortable with problems I don't know how to solve. I can disguise this shortcoming by working harder.

My Higher Power says I need to trust him more. A good exercise is for me to leave things unfinished, to experiment with experiencing the discomfort of loose ends. When I try this, I see I live to tell about it, that my world doesn't end. Making control my Higher Power only hurts me.

An affirmation to help me is this: "It is ok to leave things unfinished. It is ok to switch gears to honor my real priorities."

Fear of Economic Insecurity   July 5

Last week, my husband got a big bonus at work. I have been reflecting on our finances and finding I'm not in fear of economic insecurity these days. Of course, this could change if we got divorced or something else cataclysmic happened, but for today, the direction things are going, I'm feeling secure.

Maybe I can relax on the work front and not worry so much about finding new clients if I'm not busy "enough?" Maybe I can stop feeling guilty that I'm not working hard "enough?" Maybe I can focus my attention on other areas of my life that are not on such solid ground?

This is extraordinary thinking for me. My default wiring demands me to be financially independent, to earn my keep, to not simply be a housewife. This opens up whole new possibilities for developing my interests or being of service to my husband.

Action Plan   July 6

I stuck to my action plan today. I had allotted 4½ hours for work today and I that's what I did. Then, I found some time because (a) one of my sponsees didn't show up for our one-hour meeting, and (b) the one hour of volunteer work only took half an hour, so it occurred to me I could do more work. My Higher Power was gently suggesting I nap. I very much wanted to get more stuff off my desk. But I didn't; I napped. Will miracles never cease?

Because I wasn't all jammed up today, I had a few more moments to connect with God, and that helps my peacefulness throughout the day.

Gentleness   July 7

Given my long history of being relentless on myself about work productivity, I needed to develop habits to be gentler with myself. In my 10th step inventory at night, I ask myself these questions:
- Did I talk to myself with gentleness?
- Did I accept myself today?
- What did I do that was nice for myself today?

I try throughout the day to find little ways to be nice to myself so that I can answer these questions from a recovered place. I also try to not mistreat myself in little ways throughout the day, because I note those as well.

Last night, after a long and busy day, I told myself I could throw my clothes on the floor, that I would have energy in the morning to face them. Such a minor thing, but so important for my recovery.

Control   July 8

Control is one of the themes revealed by my step work:

I.   I feel out of control when I'm being criticized or I'm required to be critical of others. I never learned how to detach where criticism is called for.

II.   I'm not in control when I'm dependent on others. I don't know how to gracefully follow up when the people who are responsible to fix a problem are not handling it. I feel victimized when the problem affects me, but I'm not in charge of fixing it.

III.   I feel out of control when people act irrationally. Sometimes, other people are mentally ill—like one of my former sponsees. Some mentally ill people don't follow the social rules, and I struggle with how to respond to them appropriately and still have boundaries. I'm uncomfortable enforcing my boundaries—it takes work and connection to God, and I'm not interested in working that hard.

IV.   In these situations where I'm out of control, I lack faith God will take care of me.

V.   I feel in control at work (most of the time), and so I would rather be working than doing most anything else.

Fun   July 9

Yesterday, I went to picnic-type wedding. I knew the reception would have outdoor activities, but I wore a dress and resigned myself to not doing them because I would be dressed too formally for such frivolity. That is my hard-wiring. I can be too straight-laced, not much fun, especially now that I don't drink.

It is a huge victory when I fight the urge to be a good girl, especially when we're talking about harmless fun. Thus, when the time seemed right, I instigated the 50-something women in dresses and the bride to take over the moon bounce. We jumped and jumped in this trampoline-like balloon and it was incredibly fun—mostly because it was so out of character for me.

Spiritual Progress

In early recovery, when I did the right thing and resisted the impulse to act out in my disease, I seemed to be blessed almost immediately with some kind of spiritual insight or movement forward. When I did the wrong thing and gave in to my disease, I seemed to take a spiritual step backward. Thus, there is an overall difference of two spiritual steps of progress hanging in the balance every time I'm faced with a choice of acting out. If I act out, I'll be two steps backward from where I would be if I resisted the urge. One step may not be enough to motivate me to do the right thing, but two steps makes it more worth my while.

Fear of Being Fired

The WA literature says one characteristic of a workaholic is a constant fear of being fired or found out to be a fraud, despite all evidence to the contrary, like recently receiving a raise or promotion. I could readily identify with this. No matter how much praise I got at work, no matter how successful I appeared by quantifiable measures, in my heart I knew it was just a matter of time before they found out about me. This was a horrible way to live.

In WA, I found people who felt the way I did. People who were highly successful in their careers. It didn't take long before I realized my workaholism lied about my competence and job security. The disease would have me tied up in knots trying to do more and do it faster to ensure my continued employment and value to my employer.

Today, I don't feel that panic anymore. I'm confident in my worth and skills. I can talk myself down when the subtle voice finds another way to hook me into urgency and crazy-making. My action plan keeps me focused on the priorities. My program friends are there for reassurance, perspective and experience.

Being of Service

Sometimes my job requires me to be in situations which are painfully uncomfortable. For instance, attending a cocktail party at which I know few, if any, people. Or taking a prospective client to lunch. The default wiring of my diseased brain will start sending me messages like "You're a loser and everyone is going to see it because you are standing alone at a cocktail party" and "You can't possibly get business from this client because you won't even be able to come up with small talk over lunch to keep the conversation going." I can convince myself of my inadequacies and work myself into such a state of panic I'm tempted to skip the function altogether. In my disease, FEAR stands for "Fuck Everything and Run."

Recovery has taught me I have to face my fears if I'm going to overcome my disease, or dis-ease. One solution that has helped me is to try to be of service to others who are attending these work functions. At the cocktail party, I can get out of my self-absorption and stop worrying how I look by approaching people who are standing alone and start a conversation. In a client lunch, I can come equipped with a mental list of questions to ask the client such as where she grew up and went to school, what places she has traveled to, what movies she has seen lately, and whether she has kids or pets. People love to talk about themselves. The fact that I'm acting as if I care, instead of actually caring, is irrelevant. The fact that I'm switching the obsession in my head away from myself and my comfort level to the comfort of others is what matters. Counter-intuitively, it helps me to be more comfortable as well, and sometimes I even have a good time.

Recovery shows me that FEAR stands for "Face Everything and Recover." – AA slogan

Written Meditation   July 13

One of my first sponsors told me about a book written by Wally Paton, someone close to early AA pioneers, called "How to Listen to God: Overcoming Addiction Through Practice of Two-Way Prayer."

Written meditation is particularly appealing to me as a work addict. I start by just writing down whatever flits through my brain, until the flow stems. I often end up with a to-do list for the day, and that is ok. When the thoughts stop coming, it is time to end the meditation. As a work addict, I love to have a written work product as a result of my meditation. The book recommends testing the thoughts against a backdrop of whether it is selfish or of service. If the meditation produced inspiration to take a certain action, the book also suggests running the bigger decisions past a sponsor or other program person, before trusting it is the voice of my Higher Power.

Competition   July 14

As I look back over my professional history before recovery, I notice how often I competed with my colleagues, especially other women. It was a zero-sum game for me: either I won and she lost, or vice versa. I never complimented my colleagues and I vied for attention from our managers. It was always about how I looked professionally, and not wanting to do anything to that might cause our managers to be favorably impressed with my nemesis. I seethed with resentments and constantly felt the victim. I was the opposite of a team player.

WA has taught me how to be a better employee and colleague. I see now the short-sightedness of my previous focus. Yesterday, one of my female partners helped me land an important new client. After we got the good news that we had beat out our *real* competition, I emailed all of my law firm partners, praising the partner who had been instrumental in the win, and I awarded her financial credit for the client.

Giving a leg up to a colleague not only makes her look better, it makes me look better. It makes *me* better. And by that I don't mean better than her; I mean better than my former selfish self.

Saying "No"   July 15

I had a situation come up at work this week. One of my clients was being non-responsive on several matters which were becoming more and more urgent. I tried to get in touch with her on Thursday. She texted me she would be available at 6 pm. Normally, I wouldn't agree to that as it impinges on family time, but my family was out of town, so I agreed. When I tried to reach her at 6, she didn't pick up. She called me when I was eating my dinner at 7 pm. I let it go into voicemail.

Her voicemail indicated her meeting had gone late, she was now available for our call, and she would be driving if I wanted to call her back. Not only did I not want to call her that late, but I didn't want to have the conversation when she was driving because she wouldn't be able to give the matters the attention they deserved and she wouldn't be able to reference various items on her computer while we talked. So, despite the urgency of the issues and my concern about getting her attention again soon, I texted her I would be available between 3-6 pm the following day. She indicated 4 pm would work, so I called her then and we had a productive discussion.

I can't describe how sober it felt to say "no" to the client by (a) not picking up the 7pm call and (b) not calling her back that night. I showed myself respect by not making myself available after hours, by keeping work within reasonable work hours, and not rewarding someone for disrespecting my time and not keeping their appointment with me.

Multiple Addictions   July 16

Although I am addicted to many things, work is my core addiction. For many years, I worked hard all day, came home and drank myself to oblivion. So, I thought alcohol was my problem. The alcohol prevented me from feeling absolute desperation, preventing me from running away from work situations.

But once I took the sedation of alcohol away, the fears and insecurities of my work addiction were front and center. So, I figured if I just worked harder, no one would realize what a fraud I was. But there weren't enough hours in the day, particularly now that I was in recovery from alcoholism and had to go to meetings and meet with my sponsor and my sponsees. I had to find a different solution.

It turns out the solution was Workaholics Anonymous. There I learned my fears and insecurities were just lies. I found additional tools I could use to defeat this deeper level of addiction. And a whole new life of confidence and joy awaited me.

Intersection of 10th Step and Sponsor   July 17

Before recovery, I was sailing through life without any concept of the tools I could have been using to process the events of my life.

Today, most nights I write a short inventory of my day, following the format in the AA Big Book. In preparation for my weekly sponsor meeting, I review my inventory pages and make an agenda of the highlights so I'm not focused just on what happened in the last 24 hours. I include the struggles and the good stuff. My sponsor says I'm really organized. Yeah, probably. But this process has helped me see my patterns and share with my sponsor who I am. It helps her to help me. It also makes our time together efficient (which, of course, as a workaholic, I love).

Surrender   July 18

Recently, I was going on a family vacation to Colorado. When we got to the airport and were checking in, I realized that my driver's license wasn't in my wallet, where I always kept it. I frantically flipped through my wallet, disbelieving what was happening, because I couldn't get on the plane, or even check my bag, without a driver's license or a passport. My husband calmly told me to quit looking through my wallet, and to take a cab home to get my passport. It is a running joke with my husband I insist we get to the airport two hours before departure, and that was the case in this instance. In order for me to get home and back in time, the stars would have to align. We live 20 minutes from the airport, but if there was traffic, it could be 40 minutes each way.

Thanks to recovery, today I have a Higher Power. I started praying, but nothing like the foxhole prayers I resorted to before recovery, asking God for what I wanted and maybe bargaining with him about what I would trade in return. Instead, my prayer went like this "God, if you want me on that flight, you're going to have to open a lot of doors. If you don't want me on that flight, well, then, you need to show me the next right thing to do." This state of mind was a calming balm in what otherwise would have been a nail-biting, interminable cab ride home and back.

Turns out, every door *was* open: a cab was waiting for me with no line, no traffic in either direction, and my boarding pass had a special, random TSA precheck which meant I got to go through an expedited security process. So, I was relaxed and not hyped up on adrenaline when I reunited with my family at the airport. This recovery is an amazing way to live. I give up the illusion of control and gain serenity.

Pausing at my Computer   July 19

When I'm at my computer, intent on accomplishing some goal, it is the best time to be reminded the work is not everything. Sometimes the computer takes a minute to load or process; sometimes I'm on hold. Here are some notes I have around my screen to read during these times, to help keep me sane:

1) A few questions:
   a) What can wait?

b) Which tasks don't demand a perfectionistic approach?
c) What can I delegate?
2) Don't try so hard: Today, know that you do not need to rely on your personal will, energy, or effort to do your work. Feel Love as the source of your power. Rest in Love's movement. Don't try so hard. Trust Love's wisdom and effectiveness as it moves through you and others.
3) My life is unfolding beautifully around me.

Self-Talk   July 20

We become aware of our own actions, words and body sensations. – The Workaholics Anonymous Book of Recovery, *2nd Edition, p. 30.*

When I got to work today, I had a very ambitious to-do list. I hadn't prioritized it—I was at the mercy of everything that popped up in my email or calendar. Consequently, when I left for the WA meeting, my disease chattered full-strength negative self-talk: "You are so worthless. Your firm is going to fire you soon. How can you think you can work so few hours yesterday, do virtually nothing today and take Monday off because the kids are out of school?" As I walked to the meeting full of conflict, I realized what I was doing and I started telling myself: "I am enough just the way I am. I do enough. God will take care of me." I felt quite peaceful four blocks later. Amazing!

Time Out   July 21

Lately, my workaholism has been in overdrive. My to-do list gets longer each day, instead of shorter. One of the tools my sponsor shared with me in early WA recovery is the hourly time out. I set an alarm at five minutes to every hour during the day. When the alarm goes off, I walk away from my work for five minutes. It is fascinating to me how often that alarm seems to goes off. I'm so tempted to just turn it off and keep working. But I know taking even a tiny break will reconnect me with doing God's will and will break the spell of my disease.

Action Plan   July 22

Yesterday my husband and I hosted a double graduation party for our kids—one graduated from High School and the other from college.

The party was on a Saturday, and I pretty much held it together until Friday morning, when I began to panic. I reached out to a program friend and confessed I had obsessed about the party all through my morning meditation. I told her I didn't see how I could accomplish everything that needed to get done by noon the next day, but also I was now coming up with new tasks to make the party better, such as flowers and decorations and a beautiful display of pictures of the kids over the years. She wisely suggested that I: (a)make a list of the tasks I wanted to accomplish, (b) consider which ones were optional, (c) consider whether I could delegate any, and (d) determine exactly how much time I had over the next 24 hours to advance the ball.

I took her suggestions. On my task list, I jotted my kids' names or my husband next to some of the tasks. When I looked at my calendar, I realized I had only two hours on Friday to work on the party because we had evening plans. I also had only four hours on Saturday, if I skipped my usual 12-Step morning meeting. So, given the limited resources available, on Friday I tackled the most difficult tasks on my list and completed them. I reconciled myself to no flowers, decorations or pictures. And then flowers arrived from one of the guests. And my sister contacted me to see if she could come over early on Saturday to help. This meant I could go to my 12-Step meeting. And the kids and my husband stepped up and did the things on my list I saved for them.

The party came off without a hitch. I kept the crazy between my ears. I didn't try to do it all myself. I used the tools and showed up to my life as a sane and sober person, and I wasn't too exhausted to enjoy it.

Meditation & Step 2   July 23

My will leads me to adrenaline and working harder instead of smarter. My will leads me to insanity. Meditation restores me to sanity by giving me thirty minutes most days to try to hear what God's will is for me that day. I have a much greater likelihood of doing God's will in a given day if I know what it is. God does not want me to run around frantically and under pressure. God's will is sane for me.

80-Hour Work Week   July 24

In our culture, it is not unusual to hear of people putting in 60 hours a week at work, or even 70 hours. If someone is regularly putting in 80-hour weeks at a job, it is hard for that to go unnoticed, and he/she might get called out as a workaholic. I didn't work 80-hour weeks at a paying job. I didn't put in 70 hours a week at a job, and almost never 60-hour weeks. But I went to college and law school at night after working all day at my full-time job. And after I graduated law school, I had kids and ran a household with my husband while working full-time as a lawyer. I got a Masters in Law in my free time. And after I got into recovery for alcoholism, I worked part-time, raised my kids, ran a household and did lots of service in AA. Guess what? That adds up to an 80-hour week. Week after week.

Workaholism is easy to deny because it masquerades as a busy life. There's nothing wrong with having a full and abundant life. The problem is when the balance shifts and the activity is running me. It is no longer a choice, but an obsession (which sometimes feels like guilt) that makes me keep adding activity into every quiet moment. And it still feels like I'm not doing enough and I'm not good enough.

Thank goodness there is a solution and when I've had enough I can break through the denial and ask for help.

Compulsion to Check Email   July 25

Even after many years in recovery, I still fight the urge to work compulsively. For instance, I often go to the gym after work. I'll do a class from 6-7 p.m. and try not to think about work too much. Then, I hit the mat for stretching and ab work. It is at this point I get out my phone and put my ear buds in, because I listen to music for floor work. With my phone in hand, it takes everything I have not to check my email to see if anything interesting happened during the last hour.

I *really* don't want to get sucked into work while I'm warmed up from aerobic exercise and prior to stretching. That is the best time to stretch. I can check my email after my work out. The more I resist the temptation to check, the stronger that muscle gets. It is a different kind of muscle, but one that requires repetitions nonetheless. On good days, I shake my head at my compulsion, acknowledge it affectionately and say to myself, "Yep, still an addict. Better keep going to meetings and using the other tools."

God-Sized Hole   July 26

When I first came into recovery, the single word I used to describe myself in my addiction was "insatiable." If a little of something was good, more would be better. If I got praise from a boss or client, I would break myself in two to get more praise. One degree made me feel good about myself, so I got a Masters and JD as well. I needed to be a star at the office, not just a worker among workers. Achievement was my Higher Power.

When I came into recovery, I found out I had a God-sized hole I needed to fill. Trying to fill the hole in my soul with anything other than God was useless—the wrong size. Money, education, kudos, food, alcohol, love—none of these things would satisfy. Only God.

So, I started to take the suggestions I heard would help me develop a relationship with God, even though I didn't believe in God when I set out. I prayed, meditated and read spiritual literature. I trusted in the people who went before me on this journey. And eventually I noticed a sense that some presence was nearby and concerned for my well-being. Today, I'm never lonely. And it is a rare moment indeed that I feel insatiable.

Video Games – Part 1   July 27

Recently, the augmented reality video game PokemonGo came out. I'm not a video games fan—usually my husband played them with our kids. But this game was different. You had to play outside. My family was playing the game and going on long walks without me. My WA program encourages me to add more fun in my life, and to look for ways to spend time and have subjects in common with my family members. This was a great opportunity to do both.

So, I downloaded the app to my phone and started playing. Soon my family members remarked on how addicted I was to the game. I played while driving. All my 12-Step meetings were in buildings designated as "Pokestops" in the game, so I could swipe every 10 minutes and get more Pokeballs and other prizes—all through my meetings. I told a program friend about it, but I didn't have the willingness to stop the behavior.

As time went by, my connection to my Higher Power slipped. My afternoon walk with my dog to the coffee shop was no longer "media free;" I played PokemonGo the entire time. I felt hungover in the mornings, and somewhat in bondage to the game. I got some willingness to consider doing things differently. I knew I had to tell my sponsor what was going on. That motivated me to commit to some bottom lines and toplines:

- no playing in the car, unless pulled over with car in park
- no playing when I'm with other people, unless they are playing
- all time-sensitive work must be done before I play (other than at the park with dogs on necessary dog walk)
- if the server is down, wait at least fifteen min before trying again
- not making special trips to go out specifically to play
- not leaving early so I can play along the way or at my destination, unless all time sensitive work is done, and calls returned

So, this is where I am today. I don't know yet whether I have to treat PokemonGo like alcohol, and I can't allow any in my life, or whether I can partake in some limited fashion, like having a food plan. We'll see.

Video Games – Part 2   July 28

I did a little research about video games and addiction. I came across an article that made sense to me and what I was experiencing with PokemonGo. One of the appealing aspects of PokemonGo is how unpredictable it is.

In simple terms, playing a video game or a slot machine results in intermittent and unpredictable rewards. Knowing when a reward is coming gets boring in the long run but games where the player doesn't know when the next reward is coming (like when, in the PokémonGo game, the player will next see a Pokémon to catch). Anticipated rewards (similarly to actual rewards) also facilitate dopamine (one of the most important 'feel good' neurotransmitters...) release in the body.–Gamasutra, 10 psychosocial reasons why 'PokémonGo' is so appealing, by Dr. Mark Griffiths, Professor of Behavioural Addiction, International Gaming Research Unit, Nottingham Trent University, Nottingham, UK

The article went on to say the unpredictability of the reward delivery is more important to the addict than the reward itself and in extreme cases, this is why gambling addiction exists.

7th Step Prayer   July 29

The AA Big Book 7th step prayer goes something like this: My Creator, I am now willing that you should have all of me, good and bad. I pray that you now remove from me every single defect of character which stands in the way of my usefulness to you and my fellows. Grant me strength, as I go out from here, to do your bidding.

I say this prayer every morning. My sponsor pointed out this prayer makes it evident God is not going to remove all of my defects, ever. The best I can shoot for is to focus on those that "stand in the way of my usefulness" to God and others. If I can at least aim to get rid of those, perhaps I could be that much closer to what God intends for me.

My Higher Power isn't going to remove any character defect without giving me something better to replace it. –overheard at a WA meeting

Drama   July 30

When I was 16, I worked at a grocery store as a cashier. I got written up several times for my drawer being off. A third time, I knew I had a write up coming, and the manager had to give me the write up during my next shift. My shift ended, so I figured I had dodged the bullet. Then he gave me the write up five minutes later. This write up would have meant a two-week suspension. I was humiliated. Rather than suffer this injustice, or get the union to contest it, I dramatically quit on the spot.

All I cared about was how other people would view it if I was put on leave as a discipline for an unbalanced drawer. As a work addict, it is of premium importance everyone think I'm perfect, and if I had to explain to people I had screwed up, then they would not think highly of me.

I then bad-mouthed the manager who wrote me up, explaining how he was the problem for not following the requirement of writing me up during my shift. I resented him for years as I did many people who, as part of their job, had to criticize or discipline me.

This kind of behavior typifies my workaholism. Again, it is not the number of hours I work, but the insane thinking, poor judgement, energy and ego I have wrapped up in my work. I gave no consideration to the feelings of the poor manager who had to deal with my drama, I took no responsibility for my actions which lead to the write ups, I gave no thought to the bridges I burned trying to salvage my tattered ego. I manipulated people to make them feel guilt or remorse and obfuscated the situation so that my shortcomings were overshadowed.

Thanks to recovery, I have been able to fix this faulty thinking, to let go of the resentment, to take responsibility for my part and to make amends for the harm I caused, leaving me with freedom and a clear conscience.

Today, I love drama, but only if it is on the stage.

Asking for Help and Step 2 July 31

Insanity is believing I have to do everything myself. Sanity is asking for help and appropriately delegating or looking for ways to get the job done that don't require me to do it myself. I can ask myself "does this even need to be done?"

Asking for help is usually my last resort. When I'm in enough pain and desperate because reliance on self has failed me, I finally ask my sponsor or God or meetings for help. Admitting to anyone I don't know the answers and I need help is hard for me, and when I fail to do it, I find more insanity in my life.

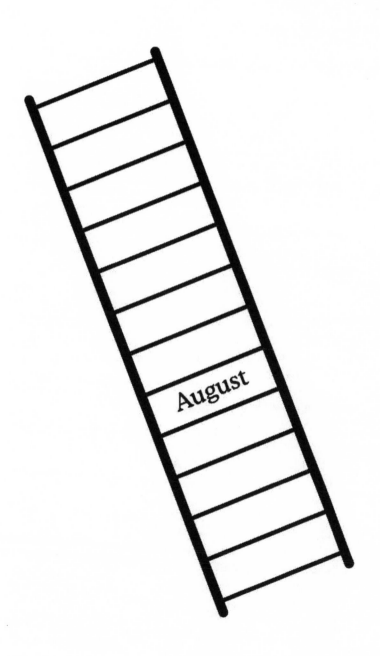

Short Time/Many Times Meditation   August 1

Before I got into recovery, I had many misconceptions about meditation. I thought in order to meditate, one needed to be in a quiet place, on a cushion, for a long period. My life was in no way conducive to such a practice, even if I had any desire to try it, which I didn't.

Along the path of my recovery, my spiritual practice introduced to me the notion of meditating for short times, many times throughout the day. I identify certain "meditation stops" which remind me to be aware for just one or two seconds. One meditation stop for me is to meditate whenever I'm on stairs—going up or down. For one thing, stairs are a good place to be present, because taking a misstep could mess up my day. Another meditation stop for me is in a movie. One might think, why would you want to be present in a movie?—it is a place to get absorbed into the experience. And that is why I challenge myself to bring myself back to my seat in the theater at least three times during a movie. I figure if I can remember to be present in such an intense situation, it is good exercise for my meditation muscle to be in good working order under less extreme circumstances.

As I'm wrapping up my day and doing my 10th step, I've noticed the days in which I feel the most serenity are those where I've remembered to be conscious of the presence of God and aware of my surroundings many times.

Time Stuffing and Prioritization   August 2

One of my character defects is trying to do everything, not prioritizing, not having perspective and thinking every problem or task is huge and urgent. This leads me to time stuff, that is, stuff one more task into every available opportunity in my schedule. I feel compelled to do this.

Recovery has shown me it doesn't all have to get done today. I won't be graded on how much I accomplished. Rather, I will be graded on how well I treated people and whether I took advantage of the journey to get to know my Higher Power.

An affirmation that helps me: "Less is more. I deserve time to figure out how to work smarter, not harder."

Meetings and Step 2   August 3

Meetings give me an opportunity to compare notes with others suffering from this disease. I can hear what is working for them. I can share what is working for me. Other members share the tools they are using and this can lead me to sanity. I can get honest about how I'm still suffering from this disease and when I verbalize the insanity, I'm one step closer to finding a solution. Meetings also give me a time out from my activities to connect with my Higher Power and the fellowship and remind me that I'm still an addict.

Step 4 Patterns   August 4

When looking over my 4th step inventory, there's no question: I am consumed with how I feel. Criticism was a theme revealed by my 4th step.

In my disease, my emotional security depends on everyone thinking I walk on water. If someone is critical or even dismissive of me, then it is the opposite of walking on water. I go ballistic. I disregard the vast evidence I am respected and liked and give a disproportionate and dishonest amount of weight and attention to one negative anomaly. I fail to understand the value of criticism: if I heard it from a more detached perspective, I could use the criticism to improve myself.

Steps 6 and 7 in Multiple Programs   August 5

When I worked the steps in my first program, I knew I would be better after working them all, and I wouldn't need to go back through them. I wondered what would remain for me to do in my recovery, because of course I was working the steps in the most honest and thorough manner possible.

When I first did steps 6 and 7, my sponsor had me make a list of my character defects, we said the 7th steps prayer together on our knees, and we moved onto step 8. But what I found over time was I needed to be in pain before I God would remove each defect. And that would happen in God's time.

On my next trip through the steps, my sponsor directed me to make a list of my shortcomings and add columns for: how the defect manifests in my life, what the opposite of it would be, and how that would manifest in my life. This, at least, gave me an alternative plan to shoot for when the opportunity next arose.

On my next trip through the steps, my sponsor asked me write an affirmation for each defect and to ask God's input about the defect and the affirmation. That was cool.

Finally, on my most recent trip through steps 6 and 7, my sponsor asked me to consider which fears have disappeared. I reviewed all of my inventories and counted up 30 past fears which no longer bother me today. What an amazing quantifiable benefit I can enjoy, being out from under the burden of so many fears. Of course, I still have plenty left, but still, it is wonderful to see progress in such a concrete way.

Depression   August 6

Some days, I'm just depressed. I feel overwhelmed with how much there is to do I can't do anything and I go back to sleep. It doesn't feel good—it's like I'm using sleep to escape from my responsibilities. Good thing I have sponsees; sometimes it is a sponsee call time that makes me get out of bed. Once I've been of service and gotten out of my head even a little, I have just enough self-esteem I can make a plan for the day. The plan might be the bare minimum I can get away with, while I take it easy on myself on the other stuff. I might still be anxious, but at least now I'm acting as if I'm not. I know ignoring tasks that need to get done will make me feel worse, not better.

The good news is, the depressed days are few and far between, especially since I've been in recovery. I can remind myself when I'm in them this feeling passes, and I just need to give myself the time and not beat myself up.

This too shall pass. – 12-Step slogan

Unsolicited Advice   August 7

Once I got rid of some of my grosser handicaps, as the AA Big Book puts it, I had to look at fine tuning. One of my character defects is thinking I know better than others about how to solve their problems, and giving unsolicited advice. I have had to work hard to overcome my tendency to do this, and of course, I'm still not perfect at holding my tongue. Sometimes I get away with it by first asking "are you interested in feedback on that?" and at least then it is not entirely unsolicited.

The person most often the recipient of my unsolicited advice is my husband. I ask God for help in my morning prayers every day for me to not give my husband any suggestions unless he asks for them. Sometimes it works. I've gotten a lot better at it.

Work Conferences   August 8

Since I've been in recovery for work addiction, my average work week is about 25 hours. This gives me the time I need to address other aspects of my life in a balanced way, such as exercise, meditation, recovery meetings, step work, service, relationships with friends and family, chores, sleep and relaxation time. However, this doesn't mean I never work more than 25 hours a week. It is an average.

Sometimes my career legitimately requires me to put in a longer work week. For instance, I attend one or two work conferences a year. These conferences present a unique opportunity for me to meet up with others in my profession and to learn about recent developments. It makes sense for me to put in 8-10 hours days for four days in a row. I briefly put other aspects of my life on hold. It doesn't mean I'm not sober. I'm conscious it is temporary, for a good purpose, and I'll get to go back to my recovery-centric life soon. It was such a relief to work this out with my sponsor so I had "permission" to make an exception. What matters in my life and long-term recovery is what I do 95% of my year, not what happens at the margin.

Vacation   August 9

As a work addict, it is hard for me to take vacations. I like the comfort and routine of work. I like the feeling of accomplishment and the kudos for a job well done. Vacations can be messy and unpredictable. It means more work to get ready to go on vacation, and more work to catch up at the office after a vacation.

But in recovery I learn vacations are important, especially for work addicts. The break in the mundane can give me the energy and opportunity to think about bigger questions in life, dream about the future and maybe make plans and goals. Vacation can recharge my batteries and refresh my motivation. Vacation gives me a chance to connect on a more intense level with my family or other loved ones.

Vacations in new locations give me memories, whereas nothing stands out in my memory when it is just another day at the office.

Recovery has given me tools to make travel more sane. Some structure helps. I have a "Self-Care Chart" with columns for each day I'll be travelling and rows I check off as I go, with the following subjects: Prayer, Meditation, Walk, Log food, Program calls/emails, 12-Step Meeting, 10th Step, Spiritual Reading.

By bringing my "usual" life routine into my trip, I can continue to feel grounded and connected to my program and Higher Power, so I'm able to handle the messiness and unpredictability of vacation.

Dogs and Babies   August 10

For the last two years, I've been driving over to my niece's house on Thursday mornings to spend 3 or 4 hours with her baby. The baby was a newborn but of course she is growing and I've been around to witness the progress from week to week. I'm not actually babysitting—I don't have any responsibilities. It's just about showing up and playing. On a business day.

I have two dogs which I take for walks three times a day. We have a deserted nature trail near our house where I can let the dogs run while I sit on a bench and say my prayers and meditate on nice days. There's something extra special about talking to God when I'm outside in nature. It feels more raw, less sterile. We also have a nearby park where many dog-owners get together to chat in the mornings while we let the dogs run. Sometimes we are there for an hour on a weekday. When I am working, my dogs are on the floor of my office, keeping me company. And the fact they need to get outside once in a while pulls me away from the magnetic attraction of my computer.

I never would have been able to do any of this if it weren't for recovery from work addiction. Dogs and babies are in the moment and remind me to be there too. It's all about joy and having fun. It is the opposite of work addiction.

Asking for Help   August 11

Asking for help is the last resort for me. It means I'm surrendering. I have exhausted all of my own problem-solving abilities and the pain has gotten so intense I'm willing to admit to others and to God I *don't know* something. This is a hard admission for me. I don't have any problem telling people about my troubles after they are resolved, but I find it difficult when I'm in the problem to admit my vulnerability. At some point, I learned admitting "I don't know" is not safe.

In recovery, I learned the only way to win the game is to surrender, ask for help and take suggestions that don't come from my own broken brain. My best thinking got me here. It is amazing how people detached from my problem can come up with all sorts of creative options I can't see. Denying myself this rich resource of help is just self-sabotage. It is so nice to now actually solve my problems instead of bury them, so I can live in serenity.

Work Relationships   August 12

Before I got help for my work addiction, many of my relationships at work were a mess. It didn't matter if the person were on my staff, a colleague or a boss. If she had a strong personality and didn't treat me as though I walked on water, then I butted heads with her, competed with and obsessed about her. I gossiped about her to anyone available. I plotted revenge or tried to make myself look good, at her expense. Sadly, this happened mostly with female co-workers.

When I inventoried these relationships in Step 4, I finally got relief and learned how to handle them more skillfully. I understand now I let my fear run the show, that I allowed these women to bully me. I have compassion for them because they were just like me and probably threatened by me. I see my selfishness in always thinking about myself and never seeing their points of view. I was dishonest because I thought their opinion of me mattered, when in reality only God's opinion mattered. Today, I don't have any issues with my co-workers, and I'm more able to work in a spirit of teamwork and cooperation.

Acting "As if"   August 13

One often hears this expression in recovery rooms. It is usually about Step 2. If I don't believe in a Higher Power, I can act as if I do and just do what I think my HP would want me to do in a given situation. The idea is if I act this way for long enough, eventually my life will start changing for the better and I will find I actually do believe in a HP and no longer have to act.

One way I can act "as if" is when I'm feeling fear around work. I can act as if I trust my Higher Power to give me what I need to accomplish the work objective. I can stop obsessing about it and have faith. I can surrender and try to identify the ways my Higher Power wants me to help myself to accomplish the goal. In this way, I stop wasting my energy on unproductive fear, and channel it into something that will ultimately get the job done.

I find it similar to the heart-wrenching movie "A Beautiful Mind" where the protagonist—a mathematical genius—hallucinates people, and the interactions were as real to him as real people. He forces himself to act "as if" they aren't there, and carry on his life, so he can avoid the side effects of shock therapy and antipsychotic drugs.

Crying about Work   August 14

If I'm in tears about work, then it's obvious I'm in my disease. This used to happen from time to time before I got into recovery, and not at all since I've been in Workaholics Anonymous. Usually, it would happen when I'd been working for a long time on some project or client and involved in solving a problem, only to have someone—usually in authority—criticize me for not doing something right. I would snap and the tears would overwhelm me. Tears are an indication I'm too wound up in my work, carrying too much ego about my role and too much energy forcing a certain outcome. Instead, I need to surrender it to God, and have the humility to see my role is simply a worker among workers. It is so much better now to have some distance from the ego and the outcome, and to be more accepting about those things I just can't control.

Being Judgmental vs Exercising
Good Judgment   August 15

I can be a very judgmental person. I think I know what is best for everyone around me. I used to go around my neighborhood and take mental stock of the deficiencies in my neighbors' property, calling myself a "blight sighter." I used to think it was my place to judge my husband's use of his leisure time and let him know when he was playing video games too much. Today I ask God for help every morning in my prayers "to help me not be so judgmental about other people." And I never even think about my husband's video gaming anymore because it is none of my business.

But judgment does play a necessary part in my life. I need to exercise judgment to make good decisions in my life. I even have to judge others to some extent. For instance, when I need to ask someone to sponsor me, I need someone who has what I want. The only way I can determine this is to listen to the prospects and make judgments about whether they appear to be successfully applying the program in their lives. This is a positive use of judgment.

Dealing with Management   August 16

As a workaholic, I sometimes have trouble understanding what is my job and what is my boss's. Sometimes I've been so involved and invested in a situation I think I know how my management should move forward, and if it doesn't go my way, I might lose my temper and say something I regret to my boss. At least, that's how I used to act.

Now, when I'm frustrated about how my management is handling a problem, I try to look at it in a more detached way: this is what my employer believes is appropriate for handling/ staffing/resolving this. Presumably, my management has a greater perspective and can weigh other factors I may not be aware of. If my company disappoints our clients or customers, then it is my employer's problem, not mine. I'm not responsible, provided I've respectfully brought the situation to my management's attention. Once. That's where my job ends. This is a much more peaceful way to run my life.

Therapy   August 17

I once had a sponsee who attended group therapy. She would recount to me all of the dysfunctional exchanges and situations which occurred in her group. I was mortified and wanted to encourage her to leave the group. I brought it to my sponsor, who noted the sponsee in question didn't have a relationship with any of her extended family. My sponsor encouraged me to think of the group therapy as this woman's extended family. Certainly, the families of those of us in recovery are often dysfunctional. I wouldn't encourage someone to cut ties with their family, so why would it be ok for her to cut off her therapy group? My sponsor encouraged me to consider therapy as an outside issue. Tradition Ten tells me that our fellowships have "no opinion on outside issues." Thus, when therapy comes up in my 12-

Step programs, I treat it as an outside issue and don't have an opinion on it.

Freedom from Resentment   August 18

At my law firm job, I had been working with Bill, the General Counsel of XYZ Corporation for years. It was my partner, George's, client. Separately, in my role as Board member for a certain non-profit, I solicited corporations for donations. I sent Bill, the client, an invitation to a lunch for the non-profit. I didn't check with my partner George first. I felt justified in doing this because I had a good relationship with Bill. George, who was a big wig at my firm, reprimanded me in no uncertain terms. I got very upset.

Here I was, trying very hard to help this pro bono cause, and George was completely unappreciative. Self-pity consumed me. Why should I even bother? I also feared financial ramifications: George was an equity partner and headed up the corporate group at my firm; he had the ability to influence my future. When I did something he disapproved, my chances for advancement diminished and I was more likely to be fired.

This all happened on Friday of a long holiday weekend. In the past, I would have taken my resentment home and nursed it for the weekend. Instead, I called my sponsor, and she encouraged me to inventory it. Because of this amazing tool, I could see my part. I selfishly did not consider George or the firm when I solicited support from this client. I arrogantly and dishonestly acted as if I was the senior partner on the client. In my eagerness to impress other Board members at the non-profit, I sent invitations to clients of my firm without checking first with the relationship partners.

What a relief! I could let my resentment go and enjoy the long weekend. On Tuesday, when I returned to the office, I went to George and made amends for my presumptuousness.

Thoughts and Feelings   August 19

I used to be at the mercy of my thoughts and feelings, whipsawed around. I thought I had no control over this. I would spend hours thinking about a problem at work, turning it over and over in my mind. I became more and more agitated and anxious.

Today, I realize that I do have some control over this. My thoughts determine my feelings. If I allow myself to obsess over a distressing work situation, I become emotionally distressed. If I distract myself with a TV show or a book, I stop being agitated. My thoughts left the problem, so my emotions calmed down. When I awaken in the middle of the night and jump immediately to thinking about a difficult problem with a client, I can pick up some program literature and calm down enough to go to sleep, instead of tossing and turning until daylight.

Pressure   August 20

When we feel energy building up, we stop and reconnect with a Higher Power. – The Workaholics Anonymous Book of Recovery, 2nd Edition, p. 30.

This is one area where I still need lots of work. But I do see improvement, little by little. Last week I was in Napa on vacation. When it was time to drive to the San Francisco airport, I allowed one and a half hours, but in fact the drive took two and a half hours, much of it bumper to bumper. Time and again the energy started building up in me, fired up by my thoughts: "It's getting later, I don't know my way around SFO, I still have to return the rental car, I still need to buy food for the flight, there's no way I'm going to have enough time, I'm going to miss my flight." That kind of thinking made me more anxious behind the wheel, trying to speed, taking risks weaving in and around slower cars.

Repeatedly, I talked myself down. I tried to change the tenure of the self-talk in my head, "You're going to be fine. You might still be able to make the flight, but even if you don't, it's not the last flight to Chicago. You will get back home. God is in charge and if you're supposed to be on that flight, you will be. If not, you'll find something else. You are resourceful and it doesn't really matter if you get to Chicago a day later." And I tried to surrender the outcome to God, which meant I still had to do the footwork to try to get to SFO, but it took the pressure down a notch and maybe even prevented me from getting into a car accident.

Once I got to the airport, I forced myself to walk instead of run, to stop at the restroom, to buy food. I walked up to the gate as my flight was boarding. Not ideal, but I count it as a victory that at least my actions were sober and I got through it with a minimum of adrenaline.

Surrender   August 21

When I do what my sponsor suggests, or take suggestions from other people in program, I often do not want to. When I do, my life changes for the better. My resistance to suggestions is my will-power. Doing the suggestion in spite of my desires is doing God's will. The more resistant I am to the suggestion—the bigger deal it is for me to bend my willpower to God's will—the more I grow. Gradually, it becomes easier for me to see resistance equals more pain, and surrender equals a good life. Slowly, I learn to trust and have faith God will take care of me. I don't need to be the one looking out for "what's in it for me?"

Interruptions   August 22

We strive to stay flexible to events, reorganizing our priorities as needed. –The Workaholics Anonymous Book of Recovery, 2nd Edition

One morning early in recovery, I came downstairs to find that my Sheltie dog, Magic, had eaten an unknown quantity of raisins—I could tell from the remains of the packaging on the floor. I had heard raisins could kill a dog. I was supposed to go to an oncologist follow up appointment at 8 am. It was now 7 am. Magic seemed to be fine. Was it overreacting to call a vet? I did a quick Google search and found a website about labs being poisoned by raisins. I recalled my brother's lab got into raisins and needed to have his stomach pumped. Was it just a lab thing? I really didn't want to miss my doctor appointment, but I also didn't want to miss the window and have my dog die because I was too inconvenienced to get her looked at. I took a moment and prayed—God, please help me understand what I'm supposed to do. The next website I opened featured a picture of a sheltie which looked exactly like Magic, and the words "In loving memory of McGee 1991-2000." It told the story of McGee eating a large quantity of raisins and dying from kidney failure a day or so later.

That got me moving. I called the vet and got Magic's stomach pumped. She had eaten ¾ of a pound of raisins, enough to kill her. We got them out fast enough so they didn't get digested. I also made my doctor's appointment in plenty of time. Thank you, God, for guiding me when I asked. I went back to the website and sent a note to McGee's owners, thanking them for sharing their heartbreaking experience so my dog could live.

We view interruptions and accidents as opportunities for growth. – The Workaholics Anonymous Book of Recovery, 2nd Edition

My Willingness   August 23

(a) I'm willing to write an action plan every day and reconcile it at night to see how my actual day stacked up against it. I'm willing to share the action plans with my sponsor.

(b) I'm willing to go to WA meetings, and participate in online meetings.

(c) I'm willing to help the people in the meetings by sharing my experience with them and being available to them for accountability/bookending.

(d) I'm willing to do something different when I feel the pressure. Instead of working with it, I'm willing to get up, walk around, call someone, tell on myself to my sponsor.

(e) I'm willing to choose the path of less intensity by choosing not to participate in a given activity which would add stress to my life, regardless of how much I want to participate in it.

(f) I'm willing to add rewards into my days—even my work days, like naps, moments of doing nothing, listening to music while not doing anything else, watching Youtube videos for fun, getting a manicure/pedicure while not doing anything else.

(g) I'm willing to listen to my family members and when they want to do something with me, I'm willing to adjust my plans so I can be with them.

(h) I'm willing to walk my dog without my phone.

(i) I'm willing to work out twice a week.

(j) I'm willing to meditate for 30 minutes virtually every day.

(k) I'm willing in my 10th step inventory to note what I have done for "fun/inactivity" that day.

(l) I'm willing to take suggestions from my sponsor.

(m) I'm willing to work the steps of WA.

(n) I'm willing to work an average 20-25 hours a week at my professional job, and write down my time so I'm in reality about it.

Image Management   August 24

When I catch myself wondering what someone thinks of me, I try to re-set and ask, "What does God think of me?" Usually when I'm in the grip of some strong emotion—fear or anger—it is because I'm concerned how I'll look if I don't get my way. Somebody is going to be mad at me. I will look bad. When I take a moment and recognize my emotion is being caused by my ego, not by the situation or the other person not giving me my way, then I'm able to ease up my grip and let God in to show me the way.

Self-seeking and ego inflation do not drive our decisions. – The Promises of Workaholics Anonymous

Working with Difficult People:

A Spiritual Solution   August 25

We remain alert to the people and situations that trigger stressful feelings. – The Workaholics Anonymous Book of Recovery, 2nd Edition, p. 30.

At one of my 12-Step meetings, a member with mental illness was driving me crazy. Jill repeated herself week after week, and she couldn't stop talking once she started. It was causing all sorts of problems in the group and a few other meetings had banned her. When Jill talked, I rolled my eyes and put my head down on the table. Then my sponsor suggested I sponsor her. I didn't want to do it, but I had found my sponsor's other suggestions made my life better, so I agreed.

When I failed to connect with God, her defects triggered me and I was full of the desire to control her and bend her to my will. When she left, I felt ashamed and dirty.

But, when I prayed before, during and after my meetings with her, to do God's will, to be of service to her, however that looked, then I could come out the other side feeling good about myself. I felt clean and virtuous when she left. During my work with her, on a good day, I was constantly checking in with God with one side of my brain while the other side was talking or listening to her.

Most of the time, I don't want to work that hard and be so connected to God. I generally want the other person to do the hard work to change to conform to my plans for him/her. The more I'm

148

willing to consult with God, and the more often I do it, the better my day goes. I learned more from Jill than all my other sponsees put together.

I don't need to avoid people who trigger stressful feelings in me. I need to be alert so I know when to get closer to my Higher Power, so I can handle those situations with grace. God for me is someone I can turn to in any situation and give my problem to. I often don't think of turning to God except as a last resort, when I have exhausted all my other resources. When I'm connected to God, nothing can mess with me.

Criticism   August 26

Before recovery, it was extremely painful for me to hear criticism constructively. It is also hard for many people (including me) to deliver criticism in a skillful way. Sometimes it comes out as the "last straw" when they are angry, so naturally, they don't choose words or timing with care. This makes it hard for me to hear the underlying message, because my ego can focus on the unkindness of their method of delivery.

Today, even if I'm triggered, I might say something like, "I'll take that under consideration" between my gritted teeth. I try to remember it is a gift for another person to tell me how my character defects affect them. I would rather know I'm irritating them than have them simply disappear from the relationship. At least then I have a choice as to whether I care to change what it is I'm doing that irritates them. When I think about it this way, I might be able to say, "Thanks for that feedback." I would like to say, "It might have been hard for you to tell me that, but I'm glad you did." And really mean it. In this way, I make it easier for them to approach me in the future.

Control   August 27

I like to think I'm in control. I'm uncomfortable when things are ambiguous, messy, or up in the air. Checking things off of my list and keeping it all organized makes me feel safe. I get a little high from it. How can this be bad? Isn't it better than my life being a train wreck? I think I deserve praise for having things so neat, on top of deadlines, acting like a grown up.

When I make "being organized" my Higher Power, my serenity is apt to go out the window when life throws me a curveball I couldn't plan for. It's better for me to reassure myself both with the big surprises and the little messes that I'll be ok even if my external circumstances aren't particularly neat. I maybe even need to practice leaving things undone for a short time while I do something unproductive, just to exercise that muscle, and not be controlled by my to-do list.

Rationalization   August 28

Journal entry from early recovery:
"I can't believe how much I want to work more than anything. I'm putting in really long hours, making up for my hours shortfall last month. I cancelled my sponsee meetings for tomorrow. I didn't brush my teeth today. I didn't meditate. I blew off my activity plan and worked nine hours instead of the four I'd planned. I fear that in letting my work addiction have this much rein, I'm disconnecting from God and I'm going to miss something He has in mind for me. It seems wrong to cancel on sponsees. But my work really did require it.

I have glimpses of hope when I consider just doing God's will. Such a sense of comfort, that it's going to be ok, and I don't have to figure it all out."

Causes of Work Addiction   August 29

Work addiction is complicated because so many different instincts trigger it in me. Some of it is a desire for money—a sense there will never be enough money so I need to grab all I can while I can. Thus, I can never say no to a client, and I have to work at high speed so I'm available for the next assignment, should it come in.

Some of it is a desire for respect and status. I want people to know I'm a badass when it comes to my profession or my recovery, and I will work hard, be super responsive and learn everything I can so I can impress all of you.

Some of it is more co-dependent, taking on too much because I want to rescue someone who needs help, or I tell myself my family depends on me financially, so I need to work more.

At different times, all of these "pressures" have fueled my workaholism.

Withdrawal   August 30

It occurs to me that I'm not a workaholic, maybe it's not so bad. This is my disease, in denial, creeping back in. I was crawling out of my skin just sitting on the train home from work. I refused to allow myself to call my associate, or write down something I didn't want to forget, or check my email. I was exercising the muscle of just being, and I could hardly stand it.

When I think I'm not a workaholic, I read the literature and see, yep, I still am.

Telephoning/Email/Text and Step 2   August 31

I use the phone/email/text to connect with other WA members and my sponsor. It is easy for me to isolate with my work and activities, and when I reach out to other addicts, it reminds me I have an addiction and there are other ways to act. All my addictions allow me to escape from my feelings or from the present, or from intimacy, which is uncomfortable for me. I would much rather work because I know I'll get a feel-good hit of adrenaline and maybe a pat on the back of approval for a job well done. This sounds much better to me than dealing with my relationships or the reality of my present moment which is probably tedious or hard.

Connecting with others in recovery restores me to sanity.

Sponsorship and Step 2   September 1

My sponsor restores me to sanity by helping me work the steps and holding me accountable for my insane behavior. She can also share her tools with me and I can try what has worked for her. Sponsoring others can lead me to sanity by allowing me to carry the message to the addict who still suffers. Sponsees show up in my life when I need a lesson they can teach me. Sponsoring requires me to stay in constant contact with my program, so I can live what I'm teaching them about.

My job as a sponsor is to take your hand and put it in God's hand. – overheard at a WA meeting

Drugs   September 2

Some people in 12-Step recovery think that if you take therapeutic drugs such as depression or anxiety medication, the drugs diminish feeling one's feelings, and blunts anxiety so we don't hit the bottom we need to recover. While I'm not taking any therapeutic drugs today, I was on depression medication for a short time when first in recovery, and it no doubt helped me stop crying every day and helped even out my emotions in withdrawal. Someday, I may need therapeutic drugs again.

Many people I come across in recovery are taking therapeutic medication and it seems to help them. Tradition 10 tells me our fellowships don't have an opinion on outside issues. Thus, for me, drugs are an outside issue I don't have an opinion on.

Filling Other People's Needs   September 3

Recently, one of my partners from New York was coming to Chicago for the first time. I have six partners in Chicago, and we began emailing ideas about how to entertain Jim. He would be here Friday-Sunday. By Tuesday, no one had proposed any specific plan, so I suggested a plan for Friday, with times and locations so others could determine if they wanted to participate.

I didn't hear anything from anyone except Jim, and ultimately, that was it. Other than one of my partners planning to take Jim to a yoga class on Sunday, there were no more emails from my partners. I was full of judgment about my partners. I felt sorry for Jim, that he had come all this way and folks were not showing up to welcome him and show off our amazing city.

I didn't have any big plans for the weekend, so I was tempted to fill the void myself. I called my sponsor and we ultimately decided that my covering Friday was more than enough on my part, and the right thing for me to do was nothing. It was so hard when Jim asked me, "So, do you know if the others are around this weekend?" and I just said I didn't know, which was true.

Although it was a difficult weekend to get through and I obsessed about him sightseeing on his own, it was right for me to stand down. So often in life there is need, but simply by virtue of there being a need doesn't mean it is mine to fill. I choose to listen to God in the process and answer those needs that are the right ones for me.

Emotional Intimacy   September 4

One of my character defects is avoiding emotional intimacy with family and friends by spending my time obsessing or in compulsive activity. If I never slow down, I never have to feel. If I constantly seek out media to provide more input (TV, movies, plays, social media), I never have time to just be with people.

Recovery has shown me that God's will for me is to have good relationships with my husband, kids, extended family and friends. God wants me to learn about emotional intimacy so I can be a good example to others.

An affirmation that helps me: "It's ok for me to share my feelings with my family and friends; it's ok to just sit with them and be and see what happens."

Financial Amends   September 5

When I was in college, I was getting ready to spend a semester in Mexico. Studying abroad meant I wouldn't have an income for several months. I was very concerned I wasn't going to have enough money in Mexico, so I started embezzling from my job. Flash forward 20 years and I found myself in recovery and thinking about harms and amends.

I estimated I stole $1000 from my college job, and with the time-value of money, I owed $3000. No sooner did I figure out the damages and make arrangements to pay it, than my husband and I won $3000 in a raffle at our children's school. It was uncanny. I have heard so many stories like this from people in recovery. It is hard to take what little money I have and pay back old debts. It is hard to trust somehow I'm going to be taken care of. It is in the surrender that I move forward in my recovery. When I leap and trust God has my back, I am amazed.

The Start of WA for Me   September 6

Journal entries

9/3/09 "…I woke up early and meditated and really heard my workaholism. Got online and started researching. Read the 20 Questions and answered half positively. Ordered the book. Only three meetings a week in Chicago. What a crazy day of to-do list. I got a lot accomplished…"

9/4/09 "…. I was dreading showering and shaving because it would take so long and take me away from other tasks. Read some materials on WA website and that adjusted my attitude. I enjoyed the shower. The means *is* the end. WA seems so mysterious—I can see I have the problem—but I don't understand how there can be any relief. Yet I know that's how I was in OA too, and turns out OA has concrete rules and quantifiable abstinence nothing short of miraculous in my case, so I have hope relief is possible in WA too. Potentially an end to worry? What might that look like? I can't believe I have to work a 4th program. But imagine my life without OA? OA has changed my life. It is worth every ounce of effort I put in. I'm actually long-term skinny and freed from the bondage of the scale and diet, and obsession about food. WA talks of not taking on a time commitment without checking with a sponsor first. There's an interesting idea. I'm feeling stretched to the limit…"

"I'm grateful for the willingness to look at my WA issues."

Grandiosity   September 7

Sometimes my workaholism exists on a fantasy plane in my head. I'll think I can create the world's best presentation and imagine all the bells and whistles and how I'll research every case and find the best clips and quotes. Or, I'll imagine how I'll read all the classics books I've missed along the way and be able to quote them. Or, I'll become an expert on some topic and write tons of articles and become famous. There's no basis in reality for my fantasies. I don't have the time to do any of the work required for these projects. I'm just in love with the idea of being the best and bigger than life, to gain respect of my fellows.

In reality, I find it unnecessary to be anything more than just another bozo on the bus, and all of my needs are met. I can do some presentation creation and some classics reading and some authoring, and that is enough. My life stays in balance because I can also spend time on other aspects that need attention, like self-care, relationships, recovery and meditation. It is humbling, but I'm glad I don't need to work so hard.

Step 4 Patterns   September 8

When I reflect on my 4th step inventory, it is clear I am consumed with how I feel and one situation in which have the strongest emotions is when I perceive I'm being publicly criticized:

- One time, my sorority staged an intervention, with my boyfriend, to confront me about what a shit I was.
- Once I was passed over for a promotion at my job (admittedly, the criticism was only implied but I felt like I was wearing a scarlet letter).

I put too much stock in how others perceive me, particularly people with authority over me (parents, bosses, teachers, powerful partners at my firm, clients). The good news is that today, I'm aware of this pattern and I can short-circuit it before it causes me to lash out at someone or do something short-sighted.

The right inquiry is "am I doing God's will?" not "what do they think of me?"

Let Go and Let God   September 9

I'm willing to consider work is not as important as I have thought all this time. Maybe achievements are not that important. Maybe doing it all and doing it all perfectly should not be the goal. Maybe I should substitute doing God's will in place of impressing people I work with. Maybe it doesn't matter how fast I respond to that email. Maybe it's ok to miss out on getting a client or an assignment from time to time. Maybe then I can stop living in fear of what I'm missing if I'm not working all the time. Maybe God has a plan that will work out better than my plan.

More From the Start of WA   September 10

Journal entry 9/9/09: "...Started reading WA book. I can relate to so much in it. How has my life become unmanageable due to work addiction lately?

- Racing at 100 mph for two hours so I wasn't late to the client golf outing, risking my life and endangering others;
- Obsession re: getting ad agency job: total excitement;
- Obsession re: Randy claiming the Ellis client, when it is mine; couldn't sleep."

"I'm grateful...

...the WA book came;

...for the dawning realization that I deserve to work out a couple times a week—that my work addiction has taken that away from me."

Merton Prayer   September 11

I put this prayer into my calendar, to pop up at noon on work days:

God, I have no idea where I am going. I do not see the road ahead of me. I cannot know for certain where it will end. Nor do I really know myself, and the fact that I think that I am following your will does not mean that I am actually doing so. But I believe that the desire to please you does in fact please you. And I hope I have that desire in all that I am doing. I hope that I will never do anything apart from that desire. And I know that if I do this you will lead me by the right road though I may know nothing about it. Therefore will I trust you always though I may seem to be lost and in the shadow of death. I will not fear, for you are ever with me, and you will never leave me to face my perils alone.— Thomas Merton

My favorite part is the recognition I have no idea if I'm doing God's will, and that it just doesn't matter. What matters is that I'm trying.

It is a test of my sobriety whether I pause for thirty seconds to open the calendar event and read the prayer. On the days I don't read it, the thinking that accompanies it is "I don't have time" and "I know exactly how my day is going to go." Those are the cocky times I need it most.

More Start of WA for me   September 12

Journal entry 9/11/09: "Reading some WA posts on the listserv. Made my first post. The beginning of a new program—so tentative, so unsure. Not knowing what to do next. The only response to my post was some fellow addict who said I didn't belong there. People don't wind up in 12-Step meetings by accident. If I suspect I have an addiction problem, chances are it is a whole lot worse than what I'm thinking it is. That's how denial works. I need to spend some time writing my "How it Was" for WA. I'm afraid I don't even recognize the signs yet. Here's what I know:

-   Not knowing how to relax.
-   Failing to see humor—taking things so seriously.
-   Discomfort with vacations.
-   Email checking at every lull.
-   Energy around work: drama obsession.
-   Wearing out my husband and family with talk of work.
-   Inability to delegate.
-   Perfectionism.
-   Fear of new situations.
-   Hollow victories: degrees, boards, speaking engagements, chairing conferences, partnership at major law firm."

Making Everyone Else my Higher Power   September 13

I don't have a boss, but there are many, many people in my day both at work and in my personal life that I try to please. Sponsors, sponsees, 12-Step committee members, other program people. Clients, partners, co-workers, staff, secretary. Husband, kids, sisters. Girl Scout co-leaders. No wonder I'm tired. I want to impress everyone with my responsiveness, reliability and wisdom. It makes me feel good when people are happy with me. If I could remember God is the only one I have to please, then my life would be easier, and my step a little lighter.

12-Step Conferences   September 14

I love to attend 12-Step conferences and retreats. My tendency used to be "I can't miss anything." Fear of missing out. Some retreats are very workaholic and every minute is full of programming. I would stay up past my bedtime and not get any quiet time.

Since joining WA, I try to do retreats in a more sober way. I book a single room so I don't have any excuse to skip prayer and meditation time. I exercise (lots of walking in nature if available), do step work if needed and take naps. I check in with my husband from time to time.

And I get to listen to thoughtful speakers with lots of recovery. It's ok if I miss a few talks; I can pick up the recordings. I get to connect with program friends, some of whom I haven't seen in person for a while. I unplug from work for a few days, so I can return refreshed.

The goal is to not need a vacation after the retreat.

Conflict Resolution   September 15

Pre-recovery, in my relationship with my husband, I kept score, compared my work load to his, martyred myself until I was at the breaking point, lost my temper, rationalized it was justified, have a fight with him, entered into a cold war for several days, and then someone (usually him) apologized. We then pretended the fight never happened, and never came back to discuss the problem. Not surprisingly, this is not an effective method of conflict resolution. It was only a matter of time before the same problem presented itself again.

Since I've been in recovery, I have learned how to inventory uncomfortable feelings, and understand my part in them. Sometimes, my part is all of it, and the inquiry ends there. But sometimes the inventory reveals that I need to confront the other person. I work with my sponsor to prepare scripts for discussions with people who I need to confront, so I am inquisitive, detached and respectful, instead of making it personal and putting them on the defensive.

So now when I disagree with my husband, we keep it short. I inventory and discuss it with my sponsor. She helps me write a script for a conversation with him. I set up a time to talk with him when we will not be disturbed and I tell him what the agenda is. Usually I find (a) I have to make amends, (b) he didn't mean what he said, and (c) the issues seem to evaporate. Some we can agree to disagree on. This is a much more productive and less destructive way to handle conflicts.

Focus on Me   September 16

One of my character defects is dwelling on the character defects of others. It is so delicious to fantasize about all the things they should be doing differently and basking in my confidence of knowing the answers. I can't wait to tell them what they should do.

Lately, I've gotten relief from this unattractive aspect of myself. When I find myself dwelling on how other people could improve their lives, I've been able to change the channel to thinking about what's on my own to-do list and moving those balls forward—even if that means more meditation, which seems like the opposite of moving balls forward. Focusing on myself is immeasurably more satisfying and brings me closer to others and God, instead of distancing me.

"The definition of love: I have no plans for your improvement." – overheard at a 12-Step meeting

Forcing my Will   September 17

I took my youngest shopping for clothes for college interviews. We give them an allowance that theoretically should be enough to cover their clothing needs. After we'd picked out a few items, I mentioned "You do realize you are paying for this, right?" They immediately became unnerved and said we needed to start over because they hadn't been looking at the price tags, assuming I was covering it. My disease piped up, telling me if we didn't get the shopping done here and now, I wouldn't have another opportunity before their interview. So I proceeded to force my will on them, pressuring them to buy things they didn't think they could afford, and effectively wiping out everything in their bank account. This errand was on my to-do list and I was going to complete it, come hell or high water. I railroaded right over their feelings of being out of control.

Later, they shared with their dad how upset they were, and he told me about it. We reviewed their spending over the past year and found it to be reasonable. I proceeded to make amends to them and we adjusted their allowance to be more appropriate to cover their needs. I explained to my youngest if there was any item among their purchases they didn't think was worth the price, we could return it and get their money back. Although they know I suffer from workaholism, I explained how this is just another manifestation of it.

I'm so lucky I have this program because it helps me realize when I'm out-of-line, and to let others know too, so I can continue to have good relations with the people in my life whom I love.

Exercise   September 18

In my disease, I consistently failed to keep promises to myself about working out. I could always justify working a little more, until the time I had allotted for exercise was gone.

When I did my 6th step, my sponsor suggested that I ask God about this. Here's what I heard: "I gave you a fabulous miracle of a machine. It is your responsibility to maintain it. Physical exercise is one of the joys I have given you, like sex and eating. Revel in it."

Today, getting regular exercise helps me feel like my life is in balance. Although I frequently drag my feet about going to the gym, I'm always glad I did. An affirmation that helps motivate me is this: "I deserve physical exercise. Working out makes me feel good. I like to move."

Pausing   September 19

I used to be very reactive—shoot from the hip, ask questions later, whip out that email in response, impulsively rush in. I heard that for every year of recovery, I get one more second of pause between stimulus and reaction. I should be up to about 13 seconds now.

This week, I did something unfortunate to my car. It was virtually undriveable—at least, it made a lot of noise, because a large piece was dragging on the ground. My immediate thought was to drive straight to my favorite autobody repair shop, 4 miles away, which would have been excruciating. I paused. I decided to call them first to ask if I could bring it in. Good thing I did; they wouldn't be available to fix it for two weeks. So, I drove half a mile home and made other arrangements.

Rest and Relaxation   September 20

Setting aside time for breaks and unstructured events without goals, we learn that there is more to life than we had been experiencing as active workaholics. – The Workaholics Anonymous Book of Recovery, 2nd Edition, p. 30.

Today I stuck to my detailed action plan. I meditated. It is so good I planned to work only three and one-half hours today, or I would have been disappointed in myself and beaten myself up. I forced myself to stop working at various points when the schedule called for it. I took a half hour lunch break and deliberately accomplished nothing. I forced myself to stop working to do one and one-half hours of personal errands. I sat on the couch for a few minutes hanging with the kids after dinner. God, I'm powerless over this fear of not being good enough.

I'm grateful...

...I was willing to stick to my action plan.

...I prioritized my work so I knew what I had to get done.

...I didn't feel pressure.

Action Plan   September 21

This week I realized I had ten trips coming up in the next nine months, some work, but mostly fun. That's pretty unusual for me. My brain started to hurt from thinking about the logistics involved. Kid coverage, dog coverage, hotel bookings. I was sure to forget something, and that's when I start obsessing. It occurred to me that, like my daily action plan, I might benefit from getting this down on paper so it wouldn't be swirling around in my head anymore. So, that night in my inventory, I made a list of all the trips, and any open questions I had (exact dates, who was going, etc.)

The next day, I sat down at my computer and put together a spreadsheet. Nothing fancy, just enough to see where the holes were, and to help myself stay organized so I didn't, for instance, book lodging twice for the same trip. It was amazing how this simple tool helped me relax and have confidence the bases were covered. This allowed me to look forward to my travels, instead of fear them.

Fun   September 22

My youngest went off to start college a month ago. They said they realized this week they had only an hour of leisure time each day. There was no shortage of fun opportunities they wanted to explore, but they felt their studies came first. They thought, "This can't be right; everything I've heard about college indicates there should be lots of time around studies to do all those extracurricular activities; I must be doing something wrong." So,they reached out to other college students and talked with them about their struggle.

They concluded the school work was expanding to fill the time they allotted to it. If a paper should take two hours to write, they said no to the fun activity to make sure they got their work done, and then spent four hours on the paper.

Their solution? They decided going forward they would do the fun thing with the confidence they would still get the work done—but they would just be more efficient about it because now there were only two hours left in which to write it.

My youngest is not a workaholic. Somehow, they were able to do what I was not—ask for help when workloads don't make sense. Before Workaholics Anonymous, I just tried to power through and sadly resigned myself to the idea that fun was for other people, not for me.

Work expands to fill the *time available* for its completion.
– Parkinson's Law

Resentments   September 23

Before recovery, resentments weighed me down. I had no clue how to deal with them, or that there was a better way. Now, when I notice I am obsessing about a resentment, I inventory it. If that fails to provide me relief from obsession, I talk to my sponsor.

It is impossible for me to be resentful unless I have some part in it. If the situation is the other guy's problem altogether, then I'm not resentful. For instance, if I returned to my parked car to find someone had hit it and not left a note, I wouldn't have a resentment because I am so clear I didn't do anything wrong.

It is in the more complex overlapping relationships of my life that inventorying is necessary to help me sort out what is my stuff and what is the other guy's. Once I have clarity, I can do something about it.

Mistakes   September 24

Tonight my husband and I were invited to go sailing on the boat of an attorney I know peripherally through work. It has been unseasonably cold, so I pulled some boots out of storage and layered up for cold Lake Michigan breezes. In the cab on my way to downtown Chicago, I was mortified to notice I'd somehow put on two different black boots. I could have turned the cab around, but then I would have been late. I considered trying to buy a new pair once I got downtown, but that too would make me late. How could I show up to this sophisticated event wearing mis-matched boots?

I took a deep breath and told myself it was going to be ok. I looked at my discomfort and saw just how much ego was tied up in it. This was nothing but image management: I wanted these people to see me as put together and in control, not a country bumpkin who couldn't dress herself. I considered just bringing up the subject myself, so we could all have a laugh and be done with it.

It also occurred to me maybe no one would even notice. Heck, the boots were similar enough I didn't notice at first. I decided to go with nonchalance. If anyone brought it up, I would admit to my humanity. If no one brought it up, I was going to assume they didn't notice. I took a picture of my boots, texted it to a program friend, and admitted my mistake to her. We laughed about my high-class problem.

I put the matter out of my head and into God's hands, nobody mentioned my boots and I had a great time in conversation with interesting people, watching the sunset against the magnificent Chicago skyline on beautiful Lake Michigan.

Ambition   September 25

A definition of ambition: an earnest desire for some type of achievement or distinction, such as power, honor, fame, or wealth, and the willingness to strive for its attainment.
My ambition is far-reaching and not just of a professional nature. I have ambitions to look good. I want people to respect me because I'm

physically fit, emotionally stable, well-read, successful, kind and loving, and a master in recovery.

I want a happy marriage. I want my kids to be happy and well-adjusted. I want my 12-Step meetings to be thriving and abundant. I want people to find my home warm and welcoming, that I'm a gracious hostess, good cook and make it appear to be effortless. All of this ambition takes me out of the present. More and more, I realize my ambition is lot about what other people think. As I become less and less concerned about that, I find my path to happiness is doing what is right for me and my family.

Difficult clients   September 26

When I did my 4th step inventory, my resentment list was filled with clients I'd done battle with. These were the people who:

-   don't pay invoices after repeated reminders, and then raise concerns about the invoices, months after everyone has forgotten the details of the job;
-   argue with me about my legal recommendations, because they didn't like the answers I provided;
-   send nasty emails, copying everyone, and then are completely pleasant on the phone and in person;
-   don't return my calls, but rage if we're not responsive enough on a weekend; and
-   are a drain on the enterprise and who take up more than their fair share of administrative time.
-

Before recovery, I thought I needed every client, that I couldn't afford to lose the income from any client. Now I know better. As soon as I identify a client as difficult, I fire them. I'm gentle with them—I suggest that they might be happier with an attorney who is more in line with the kind of service they seem to need. This frees me up not only from a time standpoint to focus on better clients, but also from an emotional and mental energy standpoint.

Life is too short to waste my energy on difficult clients.

Accountability September 27

Accountability is a tool I have found to be extremely effective in my recovery. When I was first working the steps, I did my step work on Sunday so when I met with my sponsor on Monday, I faced her with confidence. In this context, although I was people-pleasing and approval-seeking, I was taking those character defects and putting them to a positive purpose—getting through the steps.

Today, I have a standing commitment with one of my sponsees: that I do my prayer and meditation every day. If I miss a day, I have to let her know. This is powerful for me. I rarely miss, although sometimes it is just out of my control.

Drama September 28

Many years before recovery, I was flying to San Francisco to chair a conference. I arrived at Chicago Midway airport before my flight left, but the airline, ATA, had sold my seat to someone else because I hadn't checked in 45 minutes ahead of flight time. And then, when I tearfully enlisted the ATA gate agent's help to find another flight out of Chicago, she told me there were no flights to SF until the next day, which would make me late for my conference.

As it turned out, she was incorrect, and I was able to book a first-class flight on United out of O'Hare. I hauled ass to the other airport to make that flight. I was furious, I wrote several letters to ATA to complain, bad-mouthed them to anyone who would listen and I refused to fly them ever again. I carried this resentment with me for years.

When I got into recovery, I took a close look at why the situation upset me so. First, I had an exceptional amount of ego tied up in the people at the conference seeing me as reliable and professional. If I didn't show up on time, they would surely think I was a hacker. Second, the injustice of ATA selling my seat out from underneath me felt so unfair; how could I be OK in a world that changes the rules on me like that? Finally, I had booked ATA in the first place because their price was much lower than United; now here I was shelling out five times the original cost to book a flight same day first class on United.

When I inventoried this, I saw I actually caused the problem. I didn't read ATA's terms of service before I booked my flight. There it was in black and white—if I didn't check in 45 minutes before my flight, ATA could give my seat away. I could see my dishonesty in blaming them for my thinking the rules didn't apply to me. I could also see my dishonesty in believing my professional reputation hinged on me showing up on time to this one event. That is just nonsense, and my addict gets off on telling me I have to be superhuman in order to succeed. In reality, my being ok in this world depends on me understanding God's will for me and trying to do it. Finally, after so many years, the resentment was gone.

I made amends to ATA, just as they were filing bankruptcy and shutting down. I went up to one of the ticket agents and said that, while she wasn't the one I had mistreated with my drama so many years before, I was sure she had seen her share of upset passengers with unreasonable demands. She was so touched by my amends she asked me to post them in the comment section of the ATA website. Morale was so low right then, they would appreciate hearing something other than complaints. I happily obliged.

Step 12 and Oxytocin   September 29

Simon Sinek is the author of "Leaders Eat Last," a book on the biology of people working together. Sinek talks about how 12-Step programs have figured out addicts won't stay sober without service to the still struggling addict. Sinek noticed when one addict helps another, they both get a hit of oxytocin, a chemical that makes us feel trust, love and attachment. And this is true not only for the two people involved in the give and take, but others who witness it. Oxytocin is not an addictive drug. It is the same chemical released when a mother nurses a baby.

By helping each other, we help ourselves. Bill Wilson, AA's founder, became frustrated when the alcoholics he was trying to help weren't staying sober. Bill's wife pointed out he was staying sober, and that was the point.

Balancing and Step 2   September 30

Balancing tool requires me to invest time and energy into other areas of my life besides work and compulsive activities. God's will for me is for me to have rich relationships with my husband, kids, extended family and friends. It is insanity for me to focus the majority of my time on work and expect to have good relationships. I will reap where I sow. This tool forces me to do some sowing in personal relationships on an ongoing basis.

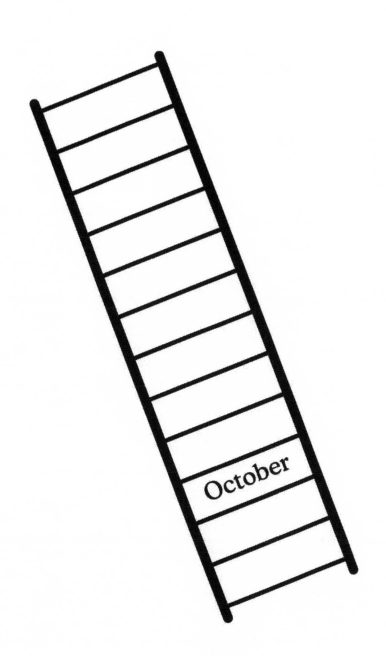

Service and Step 2   October 1

Service can restore me to sanity by helping me get out of my head and do something that is not selfish. Service can benefit one person or many in the 12-Step fellowship, but mostly it benefits me by making me useful, instead of using.

Ask not what the world needs, ask rather what makes your heart sing, and go do that, for what the world needs is people with hearts that sing. —Philip Thatcher

Confrontation   October 2

In my meditation sitting group this week I was frustrated with someone using lots of "you statements." She said things like, "When you find your mind wandering, you can bring your thoughts back to the present." The substance of her comments was perfectly appropriate, but her language got in the way of my hearing her because she wasn't using "I statements." I'm sure she didn't intend this. Probably what she meant was not to be talking about me, but rather "When a person finds his mind wandering..."

In the past, before recovery, I would have just let it go and nursed my resentment, not wanting to make an enemy. Because of recovery, I know how dangerous resentment is. Still, I debated whether and how I should say something to her. I wouldn't say something during the meeting, because I didn't want to embarrass her. I thought about sending her a text message later, but I'm also aware through my recovery work it is best to speak to people in person wherever possible if I'm delivering criticism. I decided to play it by ear: if I had an opportunity after the meeting where I could approach her without anyone nearby, I would take it.

As it turned out, I did have the opportunity so I asked if she would be open to some feedback. She enthusiastically agreed. I told her how helpful I found her comments in the group, but I thought she could be even more effective if she tried to speak more directly from her experience and perspective and didn't use so many "you statements." She said I wasn't the first person to suggest this and she appreciated the reminder.

I was so glad I had decided to risk someone being mad at me in favor of increasing intimacy and asking for what I wanted in a relationship. I felt self-esteem because I had been honest and advocated for myself. I think I was useful not only to this person, but to the group. Maybe other members were thinking the same thing, or maybe they didn't even understand what it was about her communication that bothered them, but just knew it felt icky.

Amends Harming Others   October 3

Before I got into recovery, I was contemplating leaving my husband. This brought up for me fear of economic insecurity—I was going to be alone and entirely responsible for my finances. At my law firm just then, we had a huge case which meant a big bonus for everyone who "made their hours." I wasn't going to make my hours. I was desperate because that meant less money for independent me. So, I began falsifying time records and putting down pro bono time for non-existent clients. I did this enough so my hours qualified me to participate in the bonus.

Of course, then I got into recovery and had to consider making amends. I hadn't actually charged paying clients, because it was pro bono time, so there wasn't a victim I could pay back. It was just my firm hadn't gotten the benefit of the pro bono hours I claimed I'd worked.

My sponsor encouraged me to make the amends directly to my boss at the firm—to tell him what I'd done. I was willing, but I was also talking about it at 12-Step meetings because I had a lot of concerns. Another attorney at a meeting suggested I speak to the Lawyer's Assistance Program, which is a program which provides support and resources to attorneys in recovery. LAP suggested law firms don't really understand addiction and recovery. I might get fired and reported to the Ethics commission, which in turn might revoke my law license.

I brought this information back to my sponsor. She kicked it up the line to her sponsor, who reminded us we make direct amends "except when to do so would injure them or others." My grand-sponsor pointed out I wasn't the only one involved who could get hurt by the loss of my job and law license; my husband and kids would be harmed. While I could explain the situation to my husband and obtain his consent, my kids were too young to understand the risk, so making direct amends was off the table. I needed to make amends anonymously. I had fabricated twenty hours of pro bono work, so my sponsors suggested the appropriate remedy to my firm and pro bono clients was to do forty hours of pro bono work and not take credit for them on my time sheets. And that's what I did. Whew!

Making amends is such a sponsor step. But this experience brought home to me that whenever an amends is potentially going to impact a sponsee's job, health, marriage or criminal record, it is best to get a second opinion.

Morning Routine   October 4

Lately I've been resentful about all the repetitive tasks I have to do every morning before I can get started on the real to-do list:
- Pray
- Meditate
- Daily reading of 12-Step program literature
- Feed the dogs
- Give them medicine
- Walk the dogs
- Shower
- Brush and floss my teeth
- Physical therapy exercises
- Make coffee

Of course, all of these chores are squares in the quilt that make up a good life, one that is worth living. If I start neglecting these tasks, I will lose the long-term benefits they provide. The problem with my attitude is I'm not in acceptance about them. In my hurry and anxiety to get on with the more interesting work, I don't want to be present to the less glamorous but necessary parts of life.

Morning Prayer   October 5

Early in recovery, I paraphrased this prayer from *the AA Big Book* (pp. 86-88) to say in the morning, out loud and on my knees. I've been saying it virtually every day since:

"God, please direct my thinking today, and especially let it be divorced from self-pity, dishonest or self-seeking motives. Help me to use the brains you gave me. Place my thought-life on a much higher plane by clearing wrong motives. When I face indecision, help me determine which course to take. Give me inspiration, an intuitive thought or decision. Help me relax and take it easy. Help me to not struggle. Show me throughout the day what my next step is to be. Give me whatever I need to take care of any problems. Help me be free from self-will. As I go through my day, help me to pause when agitated or doubtful and ask you for the right thought or action. Help me to realize I am no longer running the show. Let me say to myself humbly throughout my day "thy will be done.""

I find myself quite amazed at how a prayer written for alcoholics in the 1930's can be so relevant to a work addict today.

Step 4 Patterns   October 6

When looking over my 4th step inventory, there's no question: I am consumed with how I feel. One of the themes revealed by my 4th step is my lack of perspective. In one work situation after another, I deemed the "job at hand" to be *the* most important thing on the face of the planet. I added unnecessary drama and pressure to my life and others. There were so many times when I could have backed off and "taken it easy" and the job would have turned out fine (and maybe better). I have an intensity about my work that often provides me with success, but in many instances, causes me harm.

Saying No   October 7

Lately I've had so much work coming in that I've had trouble keeping up. For the first time in my career, I've made a decision to stop taking new clients, at least temporarily. I spoke with one of my partners who does work similar to mine, and I obtained his approval to refer any new clients to him. I will still get a finder's fee, but he will do the work. This is very scary for me. I take a risk that if the prospective client doesn't get me, they may find someone else, and I have to be okay with possibly missing out on some clients. It is scary for me to think of my partner not servicing the clients the exact way I would.

I have now referred four new clients to my partner. I am freed up from accommodating anyone who calls. My Higher Power is abundant and there is more than enough work to go around.

Compulsive Working   October 8

Work was so gratifying today, I didn't want it to end. When I picked up my youngest from school, I couldn't wait to get them settled in at home so I could go back to my work as soon as possible. This is so sick. I forced myself away from it long enough to make them a snack and to watch TV with them for half an hour. When our show was over and they began another, I gave in and let myself go back to my computer to work.

I'm not doing God's will when I get this way. It is so clearly my will.

I thank God for the awareness I have today that this behavior is not ideal, and accept I'm recovering with progress, not perfection.

More will be revealed. – 12-Step slogan

Ambition   October 9

My husband and I both have professional degrees and work in careers which lend themselves to 70 hour workweeks, and we are both ambitious. Before I got into recovery, we skirmished over who would compromise their day to pick up or drop off the kids at day care. We took full advantage of the day care center's hours of 7 am to 6 pm.

After our second child came along, we decided the only way to tackle running a household with two kids would be for one of us to work part-time. One of us needed to pull back on the career. Given our culture and job situations, we decided it made most sense for me to go part-time. This just about killed me. I knew this was the death knell for my career. Everyone would think I wasn't a serious attorney, when I couldn't have been more serious about my work and ambition.

It turned out my fears were not realized and I had a fulfilling career even though it was part-time. It didn't kill me or my career. Technology made it easy to be available even when I was at my kids' ball games or getting my nails done. Most of my clients and partners don't even know. I'm responsible, flexible and show up when I say I will. It doesn't matter if other people think I'm not a serious attorney; God and I know I am good at my job.

As I got into recovery, I became more comfortable with my role as a part-time attorney. I think my husband is a little jealous of my free time now that the kids are older. That difficult decision we made way back when worked out nicely for me.

People Pleasing   October 10

My Step 3 work revealed a profound people pleaser. That's why legal work is so appealing--so many clients and partners to please. And recovery work is also appealing, what with the sponsors, sponsees, people in meetings. My task will be to start turning away from the hit I get from others' approval as a motivation and turn to God instead. Wow, that will be hard.

People pleasing got me through the steps the first time. The only reason I showed up at my sponsor's house with my step work completed was to impress her. But its time has now passed. I need to grow up and be honest about that addiction.

People pleasing sets me up for a collision. What if I've done all the right things and the outcome doesn't go right? If people aren't pleased, I need to still be ok. I can't depend on their approval.

I think I'm powerless over my people pleasing. I've never tried to not people please, so I don't know for sure. I need to be checking in with myself about every decision: why am I doing this? Will it win me approval from someone? Score points? Make me look good? This is a core character defect, going back a long way.

Action Plan   October 11

On Sunday, I was feeling a lot of pressure about all the things I needed to accomplish by the end of the week, and I couldn't fathom how I could make it all happen. One of the activities included my son coming home from college on Friday with ten of his friends, to spend four nights in Chicago in our basement. This meant borrowing inflatable mattresses from the neighbors, laying in groceries and making some food. Simply using my daily action plan wasn't going to cut it, because I was busy all day Sunday. I also had fun plans that would take up most of Thursday and Friday, but my anxiety was growing to the point where I considered backing out of those plans.

So, I set up an action plan for the week. I wrote down each day and filled in the commitments I knew about already. I noticed that Tuesday and Wednesday had some promising blank space, so I immediately felt relief. I could take the time on Sunday to just text the neighbors about whether they had mattresses and set up arrangements for me to stop by. I could get started on a grocery order. Looks like my Thursday and Friday fun might be safe after all.

Fears October 12

I have been working on my fear inventory in my 4th step. I had been thinking my fear was all a lack of trust in God, but I'm seeing now all I care about is not being embarrassed. Where does that come from? Why does it have so much power over me?

I looked again at my major resentments, and in each case, someone had humiliated me. I look again at my major fears, and in each case, I was afraid someone was going to humiliate me. My fear of humiliation overshadows all rational assessment of the reality of the situation, like my proven capabilities to handle it.

If I can grasp when I'm in fear that what I'm looking at is a lack of humility, I may be able to find the courage to ignore it. I am hopeful finally.

Writing October 13

The writing process can be very healing because more than any other tool of our program, it gets us in touch with our true feelings. Writing clarifies emotions. The Twelve Steps and Twelve Traditions of Overeaters Anonymous, p. 71

I use the tool of writing in numerous ways:

(1) Inventories on my resentments: Writing helps me clarify what the issues are, how I might be overreacting due to old triggers, helps me figure out whether I need to do something further to resolve the problem.

(2) My nightly inventory: I write out how my day went. The recollection and writing process causes me to reflect on what I could have done better, who I might owe amends to, and where further inventorying or talking with my sponsor might be indicated.

(3) My amends letters: Writing out the harms and the amends helps me clarify my part and achieve willingness to make the amends and change my behavior.

(4) Scripts for difficult discussions: When I need to have a difficult discussion with someone, it helps me to write it out in advance, and maybe run it by my sponsor. In this way, I can clarify what the issues are, make it more succinct, and understand what I want from the other person. Writing and discussion with my

sponsor helps move it to language the other person can hear, instead of me just ranting.

(5) Letters to God: Sometimes, a problem is just so consuming I feel compelled to write a letter to God about it. Here, I can be more honest than I might with anyone else. I don't have to manage my image or choose words carefully. Sometimes, this results in a deeper awareness of my character defects, which might ultimately lead to the resolution of the issue.

Humility   October 14

Today after a 12-Step meeting, I turned on my phone and there was a flattering message from one of the ladies who had attended a meeting with me the day before. Then Joan from today's meeting called to ask my advice on something. Then Mary called to thank me for sharing my amends story about a former boss at today's meeting. I was feeling pretty heady. I was reminded of an AA story in which the famous Clancy I. does all kinds of nice acts and then jokingly asks himself "Is there no end to your goodness?"

I can see that the better my life gets and the more recovery I have, the greater the challenge of humility will be. How can I increase my humility? Conscious contact, for one. Constantly recognizing that everything good in my life is because of God, not anything special I've done. Me, I would have fucked it up big time if left to my own devices.

Pausing   October 15

At the start of each 12-Step meeting, the leader usually requests a moment of silence. My first sponsor told me she uses that moment for two purposes: to turn off her cell phone and to say to herself "Everything is exactly how it should be."

I don't know about others, but when I came into recovery, my life didn't feel like everything was exactly as it should be. It felt like everything was a train wreck. Wrapping my mind around that concept was hard. But I was willing to allow just the tiniest possibility that my life had come to this dramatic self-destruction to get my attention to start doing things a different way.

Today, at my 12-Step meetings, I still think to myself "Everything is exactly as it should be" during the opening moments of silence. Of course, it is easier now, when things are going so much better. Things *should* be this way. However, I'm sure they will go off track again as, for instance, loved ones in my life go through their own dramatic self-destruction, and again I will need the reminder that this is what is necessary for growth.

Obsession   October 16

I woke up in the middle of the night with my mind churning with plans for Thanksgiving weekend. As soon as I realized I was obsessing, I told myself, "Planning for Thanksgiving can happen starting November 1." Something about giving a definite date to an intrusive thought helps me to stop thinking about it, I guess because my disease is satisfied I will get back to it.

Instead of obsessing, I gently suggested to myself to make friends with now. What in this moment is lacking? There is nothing to escape. I'm in a comfortable house, sleeping in a comfortable bed with my snuggly husband and dog. My body is not in any pain, or even discomfort. My action plan for tomorrow is written down and reflects a manageable amount of activity. Be here. Be now. Sleep comes.

Recovery   October 17

They say we are always in recovery from our addictions, we are never recovered. In an OA daily reader *For Today*, it says *"Repetition is the only form of permanence that nature can achieve."* So, I can't guarantee my abstinence from my addictions, but for today, here are the actions I take repeatedly to help achieve some permanence:

- Pray, out loud on my knees in the morning and night.
- Meditate 30 minutes a day.
- Try to be aware/conscious many short times during the day, instead of constantly consumed with what I'm doing.
- Read two daily meditation readers every morning.
- Write down my food every day and eat healthy food every day. I don't eat sugar, caffeine or alcohol.
- Write an action plan Mon-Fri, and sometimes on the weekends.
- Write down how much time I spend working every day.
- Go to four 12-Step meetings most weeks.
- Attend a meditation class weekly.

- Work out two times a week and walk 5-10,000 steps a day.
- Take care of medical issues as they arise.
- Actively sponsor about six people.
- Take phone calls from people in program or I return their calls promptly.
- Take service positions in my meetings.
- Meet with my sponsor weekly, or if that isn't possible, I call her when tough stuff comes up.
- Write a nightly inventory.
- Do a 4-column inventory when I feel resentments.
- Make amends promptly.
- Don't gossip and I keep confidences.
- Get 7-8 hours of sleep every night.

We are what we repeatedly do. –Aristotle

Working Through Lunch   October 18

Once again, I compulsively worked through lunch at my desk. This has happened many days. I'm just unwilling to give up that half an hour of productivity. It is so hard for me to believe taking the break will somehow put me in a better position than working. Yet everything I read and hear tells me it is true. I need to take it on faith.

Emotional Security   October 19

The man who looks for security, even in the mind, is like a man who would chop off his limbs in order to have artificial ones which will give him no pain or trouble. –Henry Miller

One thing evident when I did my first 4th step was protecting my emotional security was the most powerful motivator for me. I would stop at nothing to ensure I would not be emotionally uncomfortable. This meant feelings were pretty much off limits. Things like fear, anger, sadness, being out of favor with someone, those were best not felt, so I avoided, suppressed and denied them for all I was worth.

Now that I've stopped numbing out in my various ways and being more aware of what's going on in my emotions, I get to feel all of the "pain and trouble." When I'm afraid and go ahead with an uncomfortable task anyway, I also get to try relying on courage, and the satisfaction of doing something out of my comfort zone. When I'm angry, I get to work through it and figure out if I need to confront the situation to fix it for the future, or for others so they don't face the same injustice. When I'm sad, I can recognize the underlying bittersweetness of love for someone who has perhaps hurt or left me.

I may not be happy all the time, but now that I'm feeling my feelings, I'm happier more than when I was guarding myself from any emotions.

Anger   October 20

I asked one of my associates—Peter—about the status of a project he was supposedly working on. He sent me a slippery email response. When I checked with our docket clerk about it, she confirmed Peter received the assignment two months ago. When I called him on it, he claimed he hadn't said he didn't get the email with the assignment, which was technically true, but his email implied he hadn't received it. I confronted him about his lying to me about a previous similar situation and sent him the evidence.

I checked with one of my partners to get his take on Peter, and my partner had the same concerns. Then I prayed before I spoke with Peter. I asked God to let me be helpful to Peter and to my firm, and to set my outrage and ego aside.

I met with Peter and encouraged him to stop working on my projects to focus on some other work he enjoyed more. My having prayed seemed to help the conversation go in a more constructive direction than it otherwise would have. We ended on a friendly note.

I haven't been that angry in a long time. The AA Big Book calls anger the "dubious luxury of normal men." I have come to find that anger can be a force for appropriate change. It is rage I need to be careful of.

Peeling the Onion   October 21

When I first came into recovery, I just wanted the pain to stop. I had made a mess of my life and I wanted to get out from under all of the problems I caused myself in my relationships and at work. Fortunately, my Higher Power was bigger than that and gave me so much more.

My first inventory focused a lot on resentments. I was such a victim. As my sponsor said, victim is a volunteer position. I learned how I had choices and I didn't have to be a victim if I didn't want to be.

Once I stripped away the resentments, my fears became visible. It seems a lot of my acting out behaviors were just masking the fears I had about everything. Without my numbing them, I was like a live nerve. Here are some examples: I was afraid of public speaking, my children dying, not being included in my kids' lives, gaining weight, losing my job, people finding out I'm a fraud, economic insecurity, looking foolish, being late, being early, endless worry with no serenity, trying new things, missing an opportunity if I'm away from work, and living with chronic pain.

They say recovery work is peeling an onion. There's always another layer to become aware of and work on. Peeling onions involves tears, in more ways than one.

Work Anorexia   October 22

I'm glad I know enough about my disease to force myself to work yesterday. I hadn't been in the office for three days. Once I get some distance from work, I start being ambivalent about it. It feels all out of control and uncomfortable. I love going to work when it is organized and I feel in control.

I hated that one of my clients had asked me questions I was actually going to have to think about and research. It was all about fear. I forced myself to analyze the client email and start putting together a response.

Today, I felt like a different person going to work. I wanted to go. I know, even though I'm a workaholic, staying home yesterday would have been anorexic and self-destructive, not gentle and rewarding. Today, I got my reward. By facing the crap and fear that made me want to avoid work yesterday, I was free of the fear, and the crap was done, so I could face my day with self-esteem and enthusiasm.

Just because I have a disease that frequently and falsely tells me I'm not doing enough doesn't mean I'm always doing enough.

Why do I spend so much of my life trapped like this, on the outer circumference of the inner richness of my own life? – James Finley

I have increased my serenity since coming into WA. Here are just a few ways:

(a)   I have experienced how the program works to solve various problems in my life, so I have confidence my current problems can also be solved through the program, by inventorying, and talking to others for their experience. I can take comfort in knowing although my dilemma may not be resolved right now, it will likely be solved sooner if I avail myself of the resources outside myself. This allows me to go on with the task in front of me and not spend my day in fear and doing self-destructive things to ease my discomfort.

(b)   Using the tools of WA. I see if I stand up and walk away from my desk when I'm feeling pressure, the pressure goes away. My disease tells me the pressure will increase if I don't keep my nose to the grindstone and get every task completed *now*, but it lies.

(c)   Meditating provides me with intuitive and creative solutions, helping me to work smarter instead of harder.

(d)   Going to 12-Step meetings.

(e)   Surrendering to working out. After a lifelong strategy of working out only to control my weight, I found OA and stopped overeating. My weight has stabilized, even without intense workouts. Now I find that I can use workouts to lessen my anxiety. My serenity increases when exercise is a regular part of my week.

(f)   Writing an action plan for my day. Putting an asterisk by those items which have to get done today helps even more. Doing the asterisked items first rockets me into a fourth dimension of existence of which I had not even dreamed.

Wisdom   October 24

We don't receive wisdom; we must discover it for ourselves after a journey that no one can take for us or spare us…–Marcel Proust

The other day, my 16-year-old's car wouldn't start. They had planned to drive their friend home. I was on an important client call and couldn't help them right then. They took my car and got their friend home, and that was ok. I helped them jump their car. But they told me they were frustrated: what if it happened when I wasn't there, or when they were at school? I dismissed their concern, because it didn't seem like a big deal. I went out to walk the dogs. And there it occurred to me maybe my youngest didn't have any clue about their options. The answers seemed so obvious to me, but maybe I could help them by sharing what I knew.

So, when I got home from my walk, I asked my youngest if they had a couple minutes to brainstorm with me ideas they could try if their car wouldn't start in various scenarios. Again, I was surprised even when the pressure was off and we were just brainstorming, they couldn't think of anything. With some prodding on my part, we came up with ten alternatives that would certainly be more constructive than going back to bed. They said they felt better equipped to handle the situation and not so much of a victim.

My 16-year-old is wise beyond their years in so many ways, I forget some knowledge just comes from experience. It is only because of recovery I could reflect upon what another person was struggling with and take the time away from my to-do list to try to help ease that struggle.

Rest   October 25

This afternoon, my family was gone and I had a number of things I wanted to get done, but couldn't figure out which to do first. I decided to sit on the couch and play with my phone until the right answer came. Turns out taking a nap was the right answer. I had guests coming over tonight, and a nap refreshed me so I could enjoy the rest of my day. Turns out the other things on my to-do list could wait.

Acceptance   October 26

Yesterday I wanted to go see the movie of the play *Frankenstein* starring Benedict Cumberbatch. It was only showing one night, in honor of Halloween. I have only been to one movie by myself ever, but no one in my family elected to join me. I left in plenty of time to get to the theatre. When I arrived, it became apparent I went to the wrong theatre. I had misunderstood the website advertising the event. If I tried to make it to the right theatre, I would arrive at least 15 minutes into the movie. I felt sad and embarrassed. I asked God his will for me. God said I should go home and not force my will. On the way home, I got a program call from someone who really needed to talk. I'm so glad I was available to her, unrushed and undistracted by a frenzied drive across town. Maybe I'll get to the see the movie another time.

And do not say, regarding anything, 'I am going to do that tomorrow,' but only, 'if God will.' – The Koran

Standing up for Myself   October 27

My car needed some work done, so it was at the autobody shop. They called me on Friday to let me know it was finished, even though they knew I couldn't pick it up until Monday because I was out of town. Because I'd been gone for a week, Monday was packed with many conference calls. At 9:15 Monday morning, I had someone drop me off at the autobody shop to pick up my car. It wasn't ready. They asked me to come back in an hour or so. I quickly checked in with my Higher Power about treating these people respectfully. I said this was the only window in my day I had available for this errand and asked if they could bring the car to me. They said yes, and to spare me the bus ride home, they even gave me a car to take home, which I later traded back when they brought my car to my house. It felt so good to ask for what I needed, and to stand up for myself.

Vacations   October 28

Years before I got into recovery, I took a long weekend vacation with my husband and friends in Key West. Unfortunately, a client wanted me to draft several contracts right then, so I worked pretty much the whole time I was in Florida, joining my friends only for dinner each night.

Flash forward to how things work today. I planned a mini vacation with my husband in Florida from Friday to Sunday, before joining my partners nearby for a retreat from Sunday to Wednesday. I did my best to get my work in order leading up to it, so I could focus on my husband and my partners and be free from worry. Just before I took off with my husband on Friday, several clients requested phone meetings to negotiate contracts that had been in the making for a while. I told both clients I would review their comments and respond via email, but I wasn't avail for a call until the following Friday. I was counting on a three-hour window on Sunday after I dropped off my husband at the airport and before my retreat started in which to do the necessary work via email.

One client pushed back and asked for a phone meeting on Tuesday and even asked if another of my partners could handle it. Neither client had mentioned in advance any urgency with the projects; they had just assumed I'd be available. I respectfully repeated my boundary and apologized for my lack of availability. Then I went on with my weekend with my husband and acted "as if" I wasn't distracted. I didn't pull out my computer during our 48 hours together, as I would have in the past. Some moments I wanted to crawl out of my skin with anxiety and self-doubt. However, I kept the crazy between my ears and kept telling the intruding thoughts "your time is 2-5 on Sunday afternoon." I had a lovely romantic getaway with my husband, and the clients carried on with the negotiations by virtue of my feedback via email on my time frame.

Fears   October 29

I feel like my fears have been quietly or loudly undermining my success and serenity my whole life, without me being conscious of them. I quit two jobs because of my fear of what others would think when they learned of that management either disciplined me or passed me over for a promotion. I almost turned away my largest client when they asked me to do a significant presentation because I feared the amount of work involved and I felt inadequate. I almost quit teaching mid-semester because I was so scared I would run out of material. I turned down numerous speaking opportunities because I was afraid I would embarrass myself with my lack of expertise and polish.

Now that I'm able to name my fears, I have taken the first step in addressing them. Before recovery, I would ignore them by medicating and numbing out with my addictions. Now, I'm trying to ignore my fears or put them in perspective because, painful as they are, I realize they are not grounded in reality.

This brings to mind the movie A Beautiful Mind, based on the life of John Nash, a Nobel Laureate in Economics. Nash is schizophrenic and sees hallucinations. The movie portrays the hallucinations as though they are real people and for much of the movie the audience is in the dark too. Nash is confronted with reality and realizes in order to get through his life without the antipsychotic drugs which make him lethargic, he has to just keep telling himself effectively "those are not real; it is my disease lying to me." Then he ignored the hallucinations talking to him. That's what I have to do with my fears. They feel as real as the actors portraying delusions in Nash's brain. But I can't believe their whispers.

Tools of WA   October 30

A journal entry from early recovery:

"I set bottom lines on Monday for email checking on the weekend. They went into effect today. I could only check my email one time after I left the office. I thought I was going to crawl out of my skin on the way home on the train. I had nothing to do. I need to carry a journal with me to write notes to remind myself to send emails, if I'm not going to be able to send them when I think of them. I also had a hard time of it from 5:15-6 at home—restless. I wanted to check email again. The time on the train unstimulated me, helped me to relax and start slowing down.

"Also, I stopped working after four hours, which was my plan, and just did a few personal items on my to-do list. I felt so peaceful walking to the train.

"This week, I committed to an action plan each day, and sent it to my sponsor, and then reviewed it in the evening to see whether my actions matched my intentions.

"I allowed time in my plan for volunteer work. I was able to do the work in less time than allotted, so I stopped feeling resentful and pressured about it.

"While there were still work projects I desperately want to do, I see they are not urgent and I need to stop working when I hit plan, or it's compulsive. I need to have time to relax. I need to get personal stuff attended to.

"Anyway, I'm beginning to have some hope that there are tools in WA that are concrete, doable and that will make my life ever so much more enjoyable."

Living in the Now and Step 2   October 31

Living in the now encourages me to stop worrying about the future, or reliving the past, and just be present to myself and those around me in the moment. It is insane to spend too much time rehashing the past because I can't change it. It is insane to spend too much time worrying about the future, because I can plan only so much and then I have to trust that God will give me what I need when I need it to do his will. It is in the now I have the chance to connect with other people and to find serenity, which is sane.

Yesterday is history, *tomorrow is a mystery, but* today *is a gift. That is why it is called the present.* - Kung Fu Panda

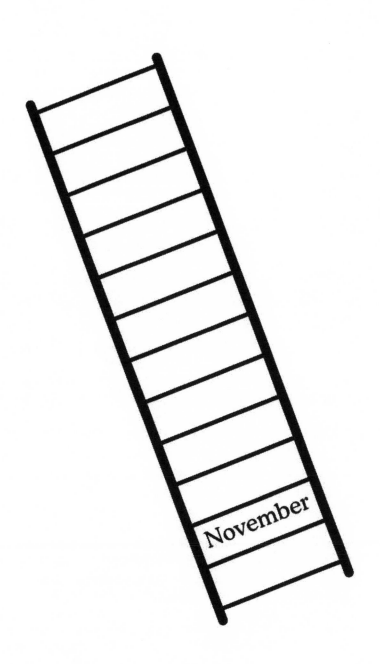

Prioritizing and Step 2   November 1

Instead of treating every demand on my attention as urgent, I can restore sanity to my life by making lists of what needs doing and prioritize my work by which ones need to be done first. This alleviates the pressure I feel. When I'm stressed, I don't think as clearly and often don't make optimal decisions. Bad decisions lead to consequences which can soon make my life insane. If I decrease the pressure, I increase the sanity.

Worrying   November 2

One of my character defects is constant worrying and a lack of trust God will take care of me.

When I was doing my 6th step, my sponsor suggested I talk to God about my lack of trust in him, and this is what I heard: "When you worry, you block my love for you, and your love for everyone. I take care of you by helping you see the next right thing to do. If you are in fear, it limits my access to you. Every little ambiguity in your life— which you chose to worry about—is an opportunity instead for you to seek me and trust."

Today, I try to catch myself when I'm worrying about the future or what someone thinks of me. I try to remember I've turned myself over to the care of God and I should act like it. An affirmation I can say to myself to help me is "I can trust God to take care of me."

Step 4 Patterns   November 3

When I completed my 4th step, I could see that I had a lot of energy and emotion around work. Most of my resentments arose when people criticized something I'd done and, instead of being open to learning how to improve myself, I made matters worse by assuming the other person was the problem. I was in denial about my humanity and lack of perfection. I catastrophized the situation and assumed it would lead to the loss of my job and my financial security.

Another category of resentments is where I fail to accept people as they are and accept that they may make mistakes. Instead of solving the problem by finding ways to accommodate others' weaknesses, I sit in self-pity and victimhood, uselessly waiting for them to change.

Here are some examples of my patterns:

- No second chances: once I have a clash or confrontation with someone that leads me to believe they don't think I walk on water, I am unforgiving. I continue to butt heads with them. I simply write them off as a lost cause and thereafter make everyone's lives miserable.
- My way or the highway: if an employer humiliates me by finding fault with my performance or passing me over for a promotion, I quit.
- False Intimacy: my feelings are hurt when I think someone I work with values me as a person, not just a colleague, and then when we stop working together, they have no more use for me.
- How will this make me look? I was always consumed with my reputation, instead of asking myself if I've been doing God's will and what is the next right thing to do.

Morning Anxiety   November 4

Sometimes I'm anxious in the morning: how will I get everything done? I try to let myself feel the feeling. Just sit there and feel what anxiety feels like in my body. I also ask myself, "What do I get out of this anxiety? What are the core beliefs behind it? Does it make me feel important to have the overwhelming certainty these tasks are very important?"

I could go to work early and start scratching the itch. Instead, I force myself not to go to work early. I pray, meditate, do my meditation readings, walk the dogs, have coffee with my husband, shower, brush my teeth and floss. Sometimes I go to a 12-Step meeting if that is on the calendar. I also remind myself this is how my disease lies to me. It tells me I have to work in order to make this feeling go away, but that is not the truth. In truth, I need to be listening for my Higher Power's will for me and trying to do it. The answer is a spiritual one.

Mistakes   November 5

I don't know where or how I learned making mistakes is grounds for self-hate. Healthy people look upon mistakes as forgivable and a natural process of learning.

My attitude about mistakes is selfish. I am consumed with myself when I make a mistake. I have no concern for others involved, I only want to do whatever is necessary to get relief from my pain.

The way I think about mistakes is also dishonest. Generally, I exaggerate the magnitude of the problem. No matter how insignificant the effect of the mistake, I see it as a mountain. I'm dishonest about my humanity, and the extent to which I am imperfect and capable of mistakes. I'm dishonest about how others will view the mistake; while they will probably be forgiving and forgetting, I am certain my reputation is ruined in their eyes.

My attitude is also fearful. I'm afraid because I think people will not respect me. I'm afraid I can't fix the mistake or fix it fast enough so people won't find out about it.

Fear and Faith   November 6

A particularly stressful day. Everything seemed to be going wrong. My son texted he couldn't figure out how to get to the University of Chicago on the train. The refrigerator leaked into the basement and ruined the guest room. My husband found evidence of rats in our yard, and the sliding back door was jammed shut. I tried to remember, in my anxiety, this is when I need to turn to God, and stop trying to muscle through on my own. I was in so much pain.

As I reflected this evening, I see, once again, at the beginning of the day, I faced what seemed like insurmountable problems. Some got worse, and then better, like my son's commute and the back door. At the end of the day, I had peace and many of the problems were somewhat resolved.

I had a lack of faith I would be ok. I thought about asking God, but I was doubtful and half-hearted. If I had had faith, I wouldn't have had the pain. The pain eased when I surrendered, like when I told myself, "If my son doesn't get to school on time, it will be ok. If he misses the train, he can take a cab."

So, lots of fear today. And dishonesty. I have seen many times before my anxiety doesn't solve my problems, it just makes me uncomfortable. Yet I dishonestly continue to indulge in it, instead of smothering the problems in faith that God will take care of me.

Obstacles do not block the path, they are the path. –Zen proverb

Acting As If   November 7

This morning I woke up feeling depressed and hopeless. Life seemed boring and predictable. Do I really have to do all this again? Brush my teeth, shower, pray, meditate, take the dogs to the park, work, meet with a sponsee, go to a 12-Step meeting, work out, eat three healthy meals, walk the dogs again, do a 10th step before bed. But I told myself this feeling of depression will pass if I just act my way into right thinking. One foot in front of the other. Just do the next right thing. And as I went through my day, doing all the things that make up the infrastructure of a good life, my depression lifted and I wasn't bored. I felt lucky to have such an amazing way of life that was no longer selfish and self-destructive, resentful and fearful. I felt self-esteem, maybe even more than usual, because I ignored the compelling voice this morning that wanted me to pull the covers over my head and give up.

Ambition   November 8

One of my partners, George, died suddenly yesterday. I worked with him on the large XYZ Corporation and the much smaller Acme Corporation. My management sent an email at 8 am asking the partners who worked with George to meet at 9:15, so we could divvy up the chore of letting George's clients know about his death and split up credit and responsibility for his clients going forward. I hadn't left the house yet, but my plan had been to be at the office at 9:30. I was worried I would lose my claim on the XYZ Corporation client if I was late to the meeting. I considered my various options for getting to the office earlier, even though I would be rushed and crazed.

Thank God I have the tools of Workaholics Anonymous in my life. When I realized I was obsessing, I asked God for the right move. I was not gentle with myself when I realized what a vulture I was being. I said to myself, "Shit. SHIT. George just died. Stop thinking of yourself. What can I do to be useful to my firm, and to the clients and my partners?" I told myself to just go to work in the way I had planned.

The *only* reason I was concerned about being late was how it would make me look and what I might lose, not how I might be hurting the firm or my partners, many of whom might really be stunned by George's death. Therefore, it would be ok if I showed up a little late. I took the train and tried not to obsess about what I was missing. I walked in at 9:30 and didn't miss the division of labor at all. It became clear to me immediately that Ben was the more appropriate partner to take over on XYZ Corporation, so I simply took over Acme. I got out of the meeting without making a fool of myself and without increasing the drama in my life. It may not have been graceful in my head, but at least I kept it there.

Self-Respect   November 9

My husband once told me it is a good business practice to fire the worst 10% of one's clients every year. They take up the most administrative time, hand-holding, they complain about the bills, and are just generally the ones that make you not like your job. Clients who aren't appreciative are also the ones most likely to sue you.

It goes against my grain to fire a client. Everyone wants more clients, not fewer, right? We work so hard to market our businesses. But I have taken my husband's advice to heart and really paid attention to which clients I like working with.

Over the last six months, I have been doing legal work for one of my partner's clients. Every month, the client complains the bills are higher than he expected. He has never asked in advance what a given service will cost. He never points to a line item on the invoice and says this particular action was not authorized. He seems to want all the work done. He just doesn't like the bottom line and complains.

At first, I told my partner I don't think this client is a good fit for me, and that clients who start out complaining about bills inevitably find a reason to not pay them. She told me she went back to the client and explained to him this kind of work costs more than he is accustomed to, and she said she had gotten his agreement going forward. This last month he complained again, and she wrote off some of her profit from the invoice. I told her I'm not going to continue working for a client who doesn't think we are worth what we are charging. She is not happy with me because it puts her in an awkward position with her client, and that is very hard for a people-pleaser like me. But I am standing by my conviction that this client will be nothing but heartache for me in the long run and I need to protect both my financial interests and my job satisfaction. If I don't show respect for myself and my work product, why should my partners and clients?

Mistakes   November 10

I found out today I may have made a significant mistake in my rush last week to file several trademark renewals in the Middle East for a new client—Jackson Corp. The client brought the matter to us at the last moment, and in our haste to get them filed under deadline pressure, we may have renewed the wrong two trademarks. I tried not to obsess. I alerted my partner, whose client it is, so the ball's in his court. There's nothing more I can do right now to set matters straight, but Jackson will likely decide not to move its portfolio to us, now. I tried to calm myself by thinking, "It's just money, and reputation." I'm afraid I've lost my partner's trust in me, and that the client won't want to work with us. I also fear that my partner won't get back to me soon and I'll spin in emotional insecurity for days.

An opportunity, right? I've tried to handle the matter with integrity, honesty and humility. Not shame myself, recognize my humanness and not pretend I'm above making mistakes. When I start obsessing, I try to keep the situation in perspective, try to be forgiving and understanding of myself like I would extend to others. I'm grateful for my progress on dealing with my own mistakes—to acknowledge them but not be too dramatic about them.

Saying No   November 11

Last year, when I went to my partner retreat, it struck me as very workaholic. We had too many substantive sessions, back to back, too short breaks, sessions ran over and as a result many people who had prepared presentations or activities were completely cut out. Everyone felt rushed and frustrated.

This year I made a point to volunteer for the retreat planning committee and thus had a small voice in the flow. The retreat turned out so much more relaxed and enjoyable.

I volunteered to organize the talent show. One of the owners of my firm suggested I put together a "Playbill" type of publication, listing the performers and including stories and fun stuff for distribution at the show. I thought to myself that sounded like a workaholic idea and immediately dismissed it, even though the opinion of this partner means a lot to me.

I herded my talented partners to commit to perform and put together a list for the emcee, a list (I might add) that changed many times in the days before the talent show, and right up until five minutes before curtain. If I had tried to nail down a program for distribution, I would have driven myself and everyone around me crazy. I'm so grateful to this recovery program because I have better judgment now and don't need to take every suggestion just to people please and curry favor with perceived authority.

Meetings   November 12

On Friday, I received an email from a prospective client asking whether I was interested in pitching a large trademark portfolio. It's now Sunday and I've been obsessing and fantasizing about the matter all weekend. Here's what that looks like:

First, the client contact knows me and my work product and has hired me previously when he was at a different company. I believe I've got an advantage over my competition because of my prior relationship with the client and his confidence in me. That's a lot of pressure. In effect, the project is mine to lose. I'd much prefer to be the underdog in a beauty contest and shock everyone by winning.

Second, the portfolio is 250 trademarks, larger than any of my other clients. It would be a lot of work to intake, as well as maintain. I'm leaving Chicago for five weeks this winter to work remotely in warm Charleston, South Carolina. That's exactly when the client would transition the work. How is that going to work? Also, the incumbent law firm may not have digital files. If they are currently using paper files, the intake is going to be even more difficult remotely.

Third, I will need someone to do administrative work to set up the status charts I use to manage portfolios. Will my youngest, who has done this work for me in the past but is now away at college, be available to work on this? Should I plan to get my son trained on paralegal work so he can earn more than minimum wage while he tries to get his career in theatre off the ground?

Fourth, can I delegate to my partners some of the legal work on the portfolio so I don't have to do it all myself? There are a lot of logistics involved in coordinating with another attorney or two.

Fifth, how will I get the Request for Proposal response done when I'm trying to be present for my family over Thanksgiving? How complicated will it be? Will the client want personal interviews with me and my partners?

I hadn't realized just how much spinning I'd been doing on this subject until I went to my Sunday Workaholics Anonymous meeting and reflected on and articulated some of this. But most importantly, someone's share at the meeting reminded me I hadn't for one second considered what God's will in all of this was. I had just been going along assuming that the goal was for me to get the client and successfully integrate and staff it. That was a pretty big burden for me to carry alone, even if I had asked my other partners to pitch in.

As soon as I remembered this wasn't up to me, that it was none of my business if I got the client, the burden eased and I could stop spinning. God would take care of it. I just needed to do the next indicated thing, which was to review the RFP when it comes in. Whew!

Too Much Work on my Desk   November 13

If I have too much work on my desk, the solution is not to work more hours. Let's say I work for a corporation and every day more work piles up on my desk because I can't keep up with it during normal work hours. If I stay late or work on the weekends, the company doesn't feel the consequences of their resource problem, so they don't address it. The work keeps getting done, so the company has no motivation to change anything. If instead I tell my management they have to choose between getting X or Y done, they start to realize my capacity will not expand indefinitely to accommodate additional tasks. They need to:

-    accept that tasks will take a longer than optimal time to get finished,
-    add more staff,
-    allow me to delegate more, or
-    otherwise shuffle the work so the load on my desk is once again manageable in the hours available.

I train my management to give me more or less work. It is not my management's fault if I have not trained them properly. If they insist I work longer hours to get the work done, I need to re-think whether the job is the right one for me.

Now let's say I work for myself and I have too much work on my desk. It is my responsibility to get the work done, but the answer is not to work more hours than is sober for me. The answer is to delegate or otherwise find other resources I can outsource to on an as-needed basis. Or perhaps I need to manage my client's expectations by telling them I can do the work next week, but not this week. If they need it this week, they need to find someone else.

Workaholics like me find the above solutions extremely painful. I don't like to admit I can't do it all, and I want the approval of perceived authority figures. I want to impress bosses and clients with my abilities and my responsiveness. If I don't give them everything they ask for, maybe they'll find someone else who will. Some of us thrive on the adrenaline generated by the pressure we tell ourselves is unavoidable and "just how things are." When I accept I'm just a worker among workers, and not a superstar, my work life gets a lot more manageable.

Vacation and Technology   November 14

One morning, on vacation with my family, I woke up at 7:30 and suddenly realized my phone alarm hadn't gone off as planned. My phone, though it had supposedly been charging all night, wasn't functioning. I was flooded with a moment of panic—on vacation on a business day and no way to check in.

Then I took a deep breath and surrendered. I could live without my phone on vacation and I could accept it as God's will. I immediately felt relief, instead of insanity. We found a lovely breakfast at the hotel. I again tried to charge my phone in the car and it functioned fine. Disaster averted.

Honesty   November 15

Here are some ways I have been dishonest:
-   Lying to cover my bad behavior, to protect my reputation
-   Stealing money from work, things from stores
-   Being passive aggressive: not being straight with people to their face, gossiping about them behind their back, being sarcastic
-   Expecting people to be able to do things I have reason to believe they cannot do
-   Believing I need X (whatever it was that day) in order to be ok, when all I need is to be connected to God and to be doing the next right thing
-   Not being honest about my skills or abilities to solve problems; dishonestly assuming I'm inadequate to handle a situation, despite evidence to the contrary.
-   Not keeping work in perspective; giving it an inappropriate importance
-   Believing I cannot be forgiven for mistakes; believing mistakes are more critical than they are

Here are some ways I have been honest:
-   Being willing to admit my addictions
-   Being willing to look at my part in my resentments
-   Not holding back anything from my sponsor at my first 5th step
-   Doing my 9th step amends to the best of my ability
-   Telling sponsees what they need to hear, and not saying things they want to hear so they like me

Accepting   November 16

Accepting: We accept the outcomes of our endeavors, whatever the results, whatever the timing. We know that impatience, rushing and insisting on perfect results will only slow any progress. We are gentle with our efforts, knowing that our new way of living requires much practice and that our best is good enough for now. –The Workaholics Anonymous Book of Recovery, The WA Principles of Recovery, p. 30

I've been asking God in my morning prayers to help me see the situations in my day as neutral, instead of assigning them "good" or "bad." Instead of looking at them as "problems," I'm trying to accept them as testing grounds for my newfound skills. I can either confront such situations trying to show up as a sober person and one who others see as an example to emulate ("how can I be useful here?"), or I can practice my character defects ("what's in it for me?"). Of course, this is more challenging the more I'm triggered. I'm having an interesting time of it on a two-week driving vacation. Many opportunities for me to practice patience, acceptance and not escalate as I have in the past. Many times to say to myself, "would I rather be right or happy?"

Martyrdom   November 17

I used to be quite a martyr, particularly with regard to my husband. I would be resentful because I had determined he wasn't helping out enough at home, and instead of talking with him about it in a respectful and loving manner, I would grudgingly do more and more until I blew up. I rationalized I didn't have time to exercise, and then I binged on food and booze because my life was "so hard." At work, I skipped lunch or exercise or put off going to the bathroom or going home so I could do just one more thing for clients, fearful something "bad" would happen if I let up for one minute.

I didn't take care of my own needs, and put others' needs first, and then I was angry at them. They didn't ask me to do this, and they couldn't understand why I was so mad.

Today, I can do it differently. I can make sure I make time for myself—what an amazing luxury—and then I have more than enough energy to give to others happily.

Illness   November 18

I have a cold. It's my first one in about eight years. I take zinc at the first sign of a cold, and this is the first one zinc hasn't worked on. I'm humbled. I cancelled everything for today (Saturday), which was hard because they were all things I wanted to do. My disease tells me to soldier on through whatever was planned and too bad if you feel like crap. I don't have to listen to that voice anymore, and I can stop treating myself like I don't matter.

Punctuality   November 19

I tend to be compulsively punctual. When I'm in my addiction, I can be obnoxious in my requirements that those around me are ready to leave on time so we reach our destination on time. I had little regard for the risks of speeding and getting in an accident. And God help you if you are the reason we are running late, because I might not speak with you for the whole ride.

When I got into recovery and started working with a sponsor on this character defect, I learned I need to take into account the nature of the event we are going to and determine the benefit/risk of being late or on time. For instance, if we are going to a party, I can relax and just go with the flow. If we are trying to make a flight, I can ask everyone to agree to allow a comfortable buffer before the flight to make sure we don't miss it. The idea is I'm no longer focused just on being punctual for everything; I can prioritize and pick my battles.

Substituting and Step 2   November 20

It is insane for me to always say yes when someone asks for my help. Pausing when someone asks me to do service or otherwise wants some of my time brings sanity. I can tell them I'll get back to them. I don't need to people please by agreeing right away. If it is a significant commitment, I can check with my sponsor and be prepared to give up another commitment. This increases the sanity in my life by giving me more choice over how I spend my time, letting me prioritize better. It keeps me from being overcommitted, which is total insanity.

Rationalization   November 21

More than any other addiction, working too much is easy for me to rationalize. Our culture rewards and admires hard work. My family benefits financially from my working hard. Given my immature, addictive thinking processes, it is just a small leap from "if a little is good, then more is better." However, I can be an efficient and effective worker without being compulsive. If I work to accomplish a reasonable professional goal, and not use it to avoid other parts of my life and self-care, my family gets the benefit of my paycheck and the benefit of my mental presence when I'm with them.

Sponsorship   November 22

Being sponsored has been a big part of my 13 years of recovery. My sponsors provided structure when I needed that at the beginning and were more flexible when I needed it down the line. I worked the steps with sponsors a number of times. I always have a sponsor I meet with once a week, to work the steps, or if I'm in between working the steps, just to check in. Although I have several sponsors, I always have one sponsor who knows everything of import in my life, regardless of fellowship.

At first, my sponsor was my Higher Power, because I didn't believe in God. She clearly had had a problem similar to the one I struggled with, and she had clearly found a solution, so she had a power greater than me. That was all I needed to get started.

My sponsor in Workaholics Anonymous had me complete the questions in the WA Book of Recovery and Book of Discovery. When I found redundancies, I just skipped the question. I typed up my answers and emailed them to her. She read them and then we set up a time to talk. She gave me great feedback on my writings and shared her experiences with similar situations. We developed a lot of intimacy, even though it was a long-distance relationship. We saw each other once a year at WA retreats.

Sponsorship is about surrender. I had to trust the things she was telling me to do (such as work the steps) which often seemed utterly unrelated to my work addiction were somehow going to help me stop acting out with work. My best thinking got me into the rooms of recovery; I had to try some other kind. And it really didn't matter who my sponsor was, just that she was outside of my own head, detached from my stinking thinking.

Thanksgiving   November 23

This is a great time of year to be grateful and count my blessings. I'm grateful for recovery and a sane work situation. For my husband and kids. For my extended family. For my relationship with my Higher Power whom I choose to call God. For my health. For my dogs. For my willingness to exercise, and how it makes me feel when I'm done. For my house. For my sponsors and my sponsees. For financial security. For my intelligence. For nice weather. For many more good days than bad days.

Before recovery, I had a life beyond my wildest dreams. The difference is now I get to recognize and enjoy it. – overheard at a WA meeting

Being in my Head   November 24

My disease of workaholism seems to find me always in my head. I'm constantly trying to work something out. Worrying, thinking, analyzing, solving. There's no question my head is necessary and thinking is a big part of my success. My problem is it never seems to turn off.

One antidote is to get into my body. Some ways I can do that are to get a massage, take a walk, meditate, take a hot bath, nap, dance, go to a spin class, take a bike ride, listen to music or go to a 12-Step meeting.

'Tain't worthwhile to wear a day all out before it comes.
– Sarah Orne Jewett

Choosing Work over Play, and Vice Versa   November 25

Last week, my youngest asked if I wanted to play a game with them and their friend. I told them I wanted to work on writing this book. I had to travel out of town last weekend and again next weekend, so this was one Saturday when I could get caught up on my writing. I realized the irony the next day at my Workaholics Anonymous meeting. I didn't want to confess it at my meeting, because then I wouldn't appear to be working a good program, but I talked about it anyway. Unexpectedly, I even started crying.

The situation reminded me of when my kids were small and wanted me to get down on the floor and play with them. I lasted about two minutes before I was picking up and straightening, putting away their clothes and toys. I couldn't just play.

Someone at the meeting suggested I let myself off the hook. The next time one of my kids asked to do something with me when my to-do list was calling out to me, I would be more likely to take them up on it. And I made amends to my youngest when I got home from the meeting.

Bottomless To-Do List   November 26

As I prepare for Christmas, I start earlier and earlier each year, hoping that this year, I'll reach that point where I'm completely shopped, wrapped, decorated, carded and baked, so I can sit in front of the fire and enjoy the silent night music and relax. It never comes. I always find one more person to buy for, one more food item to create, one more person I forgot to send a card to. On and on until New Years. The Christmas season is a microcosm of my life in general. The to-do list is never done. I have "experience greed" and want to do it all, read it all, watch it all, travel to all the places.

One year I binge-wrapped presents for four hours straight. After the third hour, I was no longer enjoying myself. I knew I should stop, I was tired of wrapping, my back hurt, but the thrill of getting it all done was too alluring. I get all hung up on the completion thing.

Today, I don't wait to listen to the carols—they are playing the first of December. They are on while I'm wrapping and shopping. I walk the dogs regardless of whether there are more items on my holiday to-do list.

Can I just say no to doing those additional things that pop up to populate an otherwise peaceful place? Can I be ok with leaving something undone?

Holidays: First Things First and Resting   November 27

Yesterday we entertained my extended family for Thanksgiving. By the time people arrived at 1 pm there was already a mountain of dishes in the sink. Reluctantly, I ignored them and turned my focus to my guests. After people went home, I put away the leftovers. The mountain, now twice as tall, was calling my name. My husband asked if I wanted to watch a TV show. My legs, back and feet were tired because I'd been standing for hours. I guiltily agreed to watch a show. It felt wonderful. We watched another. Then I did the dishes. That also felt good. I was so proud of myself I didn't do the dishes during the four hours my family was over, and I also didn't do them when I was tired. It's hard to resist the programming that whispers I shouldn't relax when there's work to do, but when I do, I'm living in the flow and happier.

Step 7   November 28

This week my sponsor and I completed review of my 6th step work. She told me my work for the 7th step is to take the next four weeks to read over my character defects and meditate about having God remove them. She also suggested a book called Creative Visualization, by Shakti Gawain. This is not what I want to hear. I want to be on step 8 and I don't want to think any more about my defects and fantasize what life would be without them. What a monumental waste of time.

But I see that my disease craves productivity, and my inexperience with this process precludes me from having faith this will work, so I will do it. I started reading the book yesterday. I often don't want to do what my sponsors tell me, but I find if I do it anyway, my life gets better. It is a way of taking step 3—I surrender to my Higher Power's will by taking direction from my sponsor.

Telephone and Internet   November 29

We reach out to stay in contact with other WA members between meetings for mutual support, especially before and after critical recovery tasks. The Workaholics Anonymous Book of Recovery, Second Edition, page 27.

Early in my recovery I discovered several email listservs for Workaholics Anonymous. Here's what I wrote one day:

"I re-entered the work world today, after two weeks off. I was dreading it, and yet interested to see if I could do it soberly...and I did! I used the tricks I've been hearing about: my activity plan, telling myself I didn't have to respond to every email today, taking a lunch break, going to the bathroom as needed, trusting God to carry the burden, and I was available for fun. I had a light discussion with my assistant, whom I hadn't seen in many weeks as she had a medical leave directly before my vacation.

I have been reading a new meditation book my dad gave me ("Wherever You Go, There You Are") and one of the tips in there is to constantly remind myself throughout the day "This is it." So that's what I've been doing. And it is amazing. So much acceptance about my life—this is it: my commute, my boring driving around on errands, my getting ready in the morning, my repetitive chores, my dog walks, my self-care, it's all ok. Not about what's coming tomorrow or the work that needs to get done. Just this moment. I never realized what polar opposites workaholism and meditation were before. One so purposeful, one so purposeless. I felt so calm all day."

Step 4 Patterns   November 30

When looking over my 4th step inventory, one theme that kept showing up was my inability to confront other people or situations where necessary.

I used to avoid confronting people with their bad behavior or their character defects at all costs. This harms the relationship—the people in my life don't know what they are doing is bothering me; my silence deprives them of the chance to change their behavior. Letting them think everything is ok is dishonest. It deprives us both of intimacy and honesty. It is irresponsible of me to let people continue to do the wrong thing—I'm obliged to address bad behavior from my staff, my young kids and my sponsees. Why do I avoid confrontation? It makes me uncomfortable and I'm afraid people won't like me as much. I don't feel likeable, and these situations trigger this core belief.

Today, I can tell people when their behavior is a problem for me. I don't do this to control them. I don't even ask them to change their behavior; that is their choice. I can simply tell them how their behavior affects me, and then it's up to them what they do with the information.

Frustrations with Staff   December 1

Lots of anger today at Betty and Ann about not getting assignments to me on time when they know I'm waiting for them. Am I just insane? God, help me to surrender my ego and anger towards Betty and Ann, and instead try to be useful, to them, my firm and clients. What's the next right thing to do?

I inventoried. Now I'm feeling humbled. I see now I was in pain because my ego was running the show. My staff is not the problem; I am. I understand that now because when I surrendered by sending the inventory to my sponsor, asking her direction and being willing to do what she says, I got immediate relief. If my staff is the problem, nothing I do could solve it. But here there was an action I could take to get relief.

My staff wants to do a good job. It is my job to teach them. If they are not performing, the fault is mine for not teaching them well enough. If I'm emotional, it is because I am at fault, not them. If I'm not detached when I try to guide them, I will miss the opportunity to find words they can hear.

My staff is a gift in my life to force me to connect with God, to be less on the lookout for myself and more on the lookout for others. I am willing to grow today and be humbled.

Under-Earning   December 2

One of my character defects is underselling myself and under-earning. I'm sure it might be hard for many readers to believe an attorney might not charge enough for their services. Maybe part of my disease is not believing I'm worth the market rate for my services. In my disease, I can underearn by not charging an appropriate hourly rate, but also by not billing all the time I spend on a matter, so effectively, my hourly rate is lower.

When I was working my 6th step, my sponsor suggested I discuss with God his will about my value. Here's what I heard: "You provide a valuable service. You went to school for many years to have so much knowledge. You have a lot of relevant experience that makes you a better lawyer. It is unfair to your firm and your family if you do not charge what it takes to get the job done. It will be ok if clients who can't afford you find someone else."

An affirmation I use to bolster my sometimes-flagging self-worth: "I am worth what I charge for my time."

Carrying the Message to Myself   December 3

Service, as practiced in Step 12, is not just to help newcomers. Doing service with other workaholics reminds me I'm an addict and have these issues too. It is important I not forget how badly I have acted out in this disease. Working with others reminds me of the tools available for my use. For instance, I used an action plan for about six months and realized many benefits from it. Then I didn't seem to need an action plan any longer--I wasn't as crazy around time as I had been.

Some time passed and I was talking with a sponsee about my experience with action plans, and I was reminded about it. I realized later as I did my 10th step inventory I had been fighting the clock all day. I kept thinking I should be getting more done, should be working on something else. So, the next day, I made an action plan. It helped me prioritize and see what could not be done that day. Now I wouldn't dream of going without an action plan every day because I see I still am crazy without one.

Meditation   December 4

My meditation this morning focused on resting and noticing the opportunities to rest in the day. It could just be a moment when the computer is loading, or at a stoplight. I found myself pausing much more today, and more frequently thinking "This is it," and "This is just how long it takes me to do this; I don't need to rush." I had moments of acceptance, even while my mind, like a wild stallion or an undisciplined puppy, was chaffing to get free. I can fight and resist, or I can accept. Today the committee in my head was willing to try accepting about 50% of the time.

Priorities   December 5

Today was Thursday, and my action plan was:
- pick up my mom and spend 9-3 visiting with my niece and her five-month-old daughter,
- pick up my youngest from school and take them to the doctor,
- go to my cycling exercise class and
- watch a show on TV with my husband in the early evening.

Because it was a weekday, I monitored my email and responded as necessary to clients. By noon, I had three requests from clients for urgent work. By 3:00, I had two more. It was almost a joke.

The old me would have abandoned my plans with my family and headed to the office. Instead, I stuck with my plan and told each client I would get to their work as soon as possible. I even did my workout and watched a show with my husband. And then I went to work in my home office from 8-10pm. And it was perfectly sober. Abstinence from workaholism doesn't mean I never work evenings or weekends, but it does mean I don't always put work first.

Wreckage of the Past   December 6

When I first came into recovery, my life was a train wreck. I was spiritually and morally bankrupt. It was as though I had been going through life in a station wagon, and when some problem came up I didn't want to deal with, I would just toss it in the back seat and forget about it. Then my past caught up with me and I slammed on the brakes. All the shit in the back seat came crashing into the front and I was covered in it. I finally had to pay the piper.

So, began the slow process of cleaning up of the wreckage of my past. I worked the steps, gained awareness of my defects and made amends where necessary. Once I had cleaned something up, I didn't have to ever deal with it again. It wasn't as bad as I thought it would be. But the only way to the other side was through it.

To-Do List   December 7

I have a to-do list for today, but I also have one for long-term projects. There's no deadline attached to most of the items so, needless to say, it contains items from six months ago. I am coming to see some of those tasks may never get done. It's similar to my attention to my character defects. When something gets unmanageable, then I'll address it, but not before. I am getting to a place of serenity about there always being tasks on my list that never get done.

Anxiety   December 8

My anxiety says lots of things to make me feel scared, but underneath it all, my anxiety is my basic human goodness exercising loving kindness and compassion for myself, in an unskillful way:

- I want you to be safe—run, you're not smart enough, and they are about to find out.
- I want you to be safe—hide, you made a mistake.
- I want you to be so safe—quit your job!

If I befriend my anxiety, see it for what it is, instead of resisting, then I have a chance of not doing something stupid. I have to hold my anxiety and reassure it I *am* safe.

Step 12   December 9

I've been hearing a lot about Step 12 at my meetings this December. Step 12 encourages me to carry the message of recovery to those still suffering. I'm reminded if I'm enjoying the gifts of recovery, I can't keep them unless I share my recovery with others. If I don't help newcomers and others struggling to get better, I myself will not stay sober. It is in the process of relaying the message that I hear what I need. On the other hand, if I don't have recovery, I can't give it away. I need to pick up the spiritual toolkit and use it every day to address the next layer of the onion. Otherwise, my life will become unmanageable and then I won't have anything others want.

If I don't have it, I can't give it away. If I have it, I have to give it away to keep it.

Technology   December 10

I'm all in favor of technology and the amazing developments we have witnessed in the last 30 years. One would think with these strides forward, we could work less and let the technology carry the load for us. But far from that scenario, the advancements in technology have increased the ability for me to work more. Here are some examples:
- I can respond to a work email while driving.
- I can check work emails before I get out of bed.
- I can stay up too late checking endless postings on social media, or binge-watching TV series on Netflix.
- I can continue to get high on work after I leave my office by checking for emails into the evening.
- I can carry on a relationship for years with clients exclusively over email.

- I give my cell phone number to work colleagues so they can reach me at any hour.

Instead of making my life easier with less work, technology allows it to creep into weekends, vacations and dinners out with my husband.

Technology advancements require I become even more vigilant in my practice of the principles of the WA program. Here are some ways I try to fight back:
- I don't email work colleagues on evenings and weekends, except for the rare emergency.
- I try to observe a reasonable bedtime to allow myself at least 7½ hours of sleep.
- I keep a close eye on my social media and TV consumption to see if it starts to cross over into a preoccupation which prevents me from meeting my responsibilities, including self-care.
- I try to pick up the phone from time to time with work colleagues so there is also a personal side to our relationships, and not just emails.
- I keep note of how much time I'm working, so I'm not in vagueness or denial.

Sponsors   December 11

"We find a WA member who is committed to abstinence from compulsive working to help us work the Steps, Traditions and Tools. Sponsors offer guidance through the recovery process on all three levels: physical, emotional and spiritual. A member may work with more than one sponsor and may change sponsors at will. We become a sponsor as a way of working Step Twelve, carrying the WA message and putting the principles of the program into practice. We ask to be sponsored so that we can benefit from the experience of someone who has achieved what we want. WA is a program of attraction, so we find a sponsor whose recovery inspires us and follow his or her lead." The Workaholics Anonymous Book of Recovery, 2nd Edition

My first WA sponsor—the one who took me through the steps the first time—lived in another state. A mutual WA friend introduced us via email. My sponsor suggested I answer the questions in the WA Book of Recovery and email my answers to her. She reviewed them

and we would set up a time to go over her comments by phone. I started working the steps in Oct 2009 and finished in April 2011. We met by phone every week or so. She gave me lots of other suggestions and assignments as we worked together, depending on what I was struggling with. For instance, in Step 1, she suggested I make a list of:
- everything in my history I considered to be a success,
- all of my service commitments, and then get rid of several of them,
- my bottom lines,
- my false core beliefs, and
- those things I consider to be rewards, and then start giving them to myself.

Vacation   December 12

A weird phenomenon happens when I go on vacation now. After four or five days away from the office, I start to imagine life without my job. I may start fantasizing about a different job. I might casually open an email from work and think, "I so totally do not care about this." It is a little frightening how much I don't want to go back to work. And yet, I know as soon as I'm back in my office, I'll be fine, my work will be satisfying and I will care again. So, it is just an illusion. It's nice that I can unplug so completely.

Taskmaster vs Cheerleader   December 13

I am my own worst enemy and a taskmaster. I have to actively fight the tendencies in myself to do it all and do it all perfectly.

I write a 10th step inventory virtually every night. Two of the questions I ask myself are "Did I speak to myself gently and was I in acceptance about myself?" and "Did I do something nice for myself today?"

Last night at bedtime I was unusually tired. Normally, I would put my clothes away after undressing, but my recovered voice gave me a break and said I could drop my clothes where they fell and deal with them in the morning. It was such a relief. A small thing, but a victory over the unforgiving voice in my head.

I appreciated being able to answer the questions in my inventory last night in the affirmative. I can be my own cheerleader.

I was preparing to give my first talk in a 12-Step meeting on the topic "The Tools." I had made a list:

TOOL No 1)	Figure out your bottom lines
TOOL No 2)	Avoid HALT
TOOL No 3)	Get a sponsor
TOOL No 4)	Go to meetings
TOOL No 5)	Consider the consequences
TOOL No 6)	Journal
TOOL No 7)	Feel your feelings
TOOL No 8)	Call someone in program
TOOL No 9)	Ask newcomers for their phone numbers
TOOL No 10)	Go to fellowship
TOOL No 11)	Be of service
TOOL No 12)	Establish conscious contact with a Higher Power
TOOL No 13)	Do step work
TOOL No 14)	Read program material
TOOL No 15)	Attend 12-Step conferences
TOOL No 16)	Use the slogans

As I rehearsed, I had a very uncomfortable feeling about it. Why did it sound so pedantic and preachy? It's like I was invested in making sure everyone in the meeting understood all the reasons why they needed to use these tools.

Then, in a stroke of understanding, I realized my problem. I needed to change them to be from my experience, not telling others what they should be doing. I swapped out the "you statements" for "I statements."

TOOL No 1)	Figure out my bottom lines
TOOL No 2)	I need to avoid HALT
TOOL No 3)	I got a sponsor
TOOL No 4)	I go to meetings
TOOL No 5)	I try to consider the consequences
TOOL No 6)	I journal at night
TOOL No 7)	I stop to feel my feelings
TOOL No 8)	I call people in program

TOOL No 9)   I ask newcomers for their phone numbers
TOOL No 10)   I go to fellowship
TOOL No 11)   I try to be of service
TOOL No 12)   I try to establish conscious contact with a Higher Power
TOOL No 13)   I do step work
TOOL No 14)   I read program material
TOOL No 15)   I attend 12-Step conferences
TOOL No 16)   I say the slogans

What a difference this shift made! I no longer felt pressure to convince others of the value of these tools. All I had to do was share what worked for me and those attending could take what they liked and leave the rest.

Self-Reliance   December 15

For as long as I can recall before recovery, I was very independent. I remember hearing the Simon & Garfunkel lyrics "I am a rock; I am an island," and thinking, "Yep, that's about right." For a long time, that served me, until it stopped working.

The AA Big Book directs me to ask myself where self-reliance has failed me. By relying only on my limited knowledge, I think I know how things are going to go, and it looks like it's going to go badly, so I live in fear. By relying on my limited experience, I don't understand there's another, sober way to do things.

By not reaching out to other people, I have so few tools with which to try to solve my problems, and I don't learn any new ones. Left to my own devices, I have no option but to trust my self-talk which says I'm inadequate for any given task, and which routinely lies. No reliance on God means I failed to tap into a significant source of comfort that I would be taken care of, and a source of courage to face difficult situations. I had no idea my purpose was to do God's will. My own resources had no way to show me that. I was a failure relying on myself because I had no inkling of the real purpose of my life. I was completely misguided. Having no reliance on God deprived me of the true guidance I needed to do the next right thing.

Self-Care   December 16

I'm grateful today for a routine of self-care. In the midst of an insanely pressured workday, I went to the bathroom when I needed to, drank my water, ate my healthy meals and snacks, and got in 40 minutes of aerobic exercise. That is a miracle. Even without the other tools of WA, I have made a lot of progress against this disease just by bringing in the sanity and balance of self-care.

Taking Sober Risks   December 17

We were afraid we would be forced to change, surrender important goals, or give up a nice paycheck. We may have liked the idea of slowing down to have a balanced life in theory, but the lure of rushing to generate intensity and cultivate a sense of self-importance was overpowering.—Workaholics Anonymous Book of Recovery, Second Edition, p. 1

When I came into WA, I was sure "they" would make me leave my prestigious job as a partner at one of the world's biggest law firms. I identified myself by that job. I was very sure I didn't want to leave it. But over the years, the program worked on me. Another fellowship promises this: *"Careers that had been exploited mainly for material security at the expense of self-fulfillment no longer appealed to us."*

Three years ago, I had the opportunity to join an entrepreneurial, virtual firm. I could work from home, in the company of my dogs. I wouldn't get a salary: my paycheck depended entirely on whatever work I brought to the firm. My sponsor encouraged me to take the leap, convinced I would be successful and I shouldn't miss the opportunity just because I was scared.

Now, at the end of my third year with the smaller firm, I worked 15% fewer hours and earned as much this year as I did at the big law firm. I couldn't be happier.

"Courage is fear that has said its prayers." —Karle Wilson Baker

Self Will   December 18

While I am presented with wonderful and exciting opportunities on my journey, it is better for me to let go of the outcome and be in acceptance about God's will, before I see/hear the outcome. This helps me get honest about my role of not being in charge. And helps prevent me from crashing if the decision is not to my liking. What goes up, must come down. It helps me to re-read the Step 3 pages in the Alcoholics Anonymous Big Book about acting and directing.

"First of all, we had to quit playing God. It didn't work." – Alcoholics Anonymous, 4th Edition, p. 62.

Exercise   December 19

I struggle with people-pleasing and boundaries. A visitor stayed over at our house for four days recently. I went to work out one evening, which was a huge victory of self-care instead of staying home to care-take my visitor. She questioned why I needed to go the Y when I had just walked the dog. I explained that a cycling class is a different aerobic level of exercise than walking the dog. Before recovery, I could never have gone to the Y with guests at my house.

Dancing   December 20

I recently left my big law firm job and joined a small virtual firm. During my tenure at the big firm, I was too guarded to let people know me. I preferred to be the consummate professional and wouldn't risk looking undignified.

One thing recovery has taught me is to try new, uncomfortable things, and to try to have more fun. One day I got an email from a partner at the new firm looking for volunteers backup singers and dancers for a talent show at our annual partner retreat. Now, I can hold a tune, but I've never even tried to learn a dance routine before. But I put my hand up and I learned some steps to the tune of "All the Single Ladies." Our practices were virtual and on our own since we lived in different cities, and we got together at the retreat to put it all together. I have to admit I practiced seriously—10 minutes a day for about a month, because, you know, I didn't want to look like an idiot.

When I got the retreat, being a part of the sketch gave me a sense of belonging. I also felt like I'd given my disease a great big "fuck you" because we had so much fun!

Self-Esteem   December 21

I have found I can't give myself self-esteem, but I need to earn it by doing esteemable acts. That can mean different things for me, depending on what's called for in the moment. It can be performing service for others, sometimes even just forcing myself to think about others, when I would rather be self-involved. It could be standing up for myself in the face of disrespect or abuse. It might be self-care. I get self-esteem when, at the end of the day, I see that my actions aligned with my intentions.

Action Plan   December 22

"We put on paper what we intend to do each day. We are conscious of the way we spend our time to ensure that we are able to properly care for our bodies with healthy food, appropriate exercise, and an adequate amount of sleep." –The Workaholics Anonymous Book of Recovery, 2nd edition.

I resisted the tool of writing an action plan for my day. I thought having my plan in my head was just fine. Then I started working from home on Tuesdays. Every Tuesday morning, I would have grandiose ideas about everything I would get done. I thought I could work for six hours, run three hours of errands, get a manicure and work out, and pick up the kids from school at 3:00. Week after week, I was so frustrated by 2 pm on Tuesdays, beating myself up because I was so inefficient. Of course, I didn't know my plan was unrealistic because I wasn't writing it down.

So, after six months in the WA program, I finally gave in. I wrote what I was going to do for each hour. Lo and behold, on paper I could see I couldn't fit in everything I wanted. I was forced to make choices and move some things to the next day. I had to *prioritize*. And an amazing change came over me. I was calm and could do things in a sane manner, without feeling pressure. I could take a leisurely shower because I had allowed myself half an hour, instead of trying to race through it in five minutes so I could get to something else. I started making an action plan every day. I write it the night before, and then I can go to sleep with a calm confidence about what the next day looks like.

Some days, even with a plan, so many new things come at me I get paralyzed and don't even know where to start. That's when I have to do a mid-day course correction. It's just a list of everything that needs to get done. Then I asterisk those tasks which must be completed today. I clear off my desk all those things I've decided can wait until tomorrow. I focus on the one or two that can't wait. That way, I'm not distracted by those other tasks. If I get the priorities done, I can again look to my to-do list to knock off a few more.

"Never do today what you can put off until tomorrow." – WA slogan

Boundaries   December 23

It's Friday, the day before Christmas Eve. One of my clients asked if I was available to revise a contract. He was getting of pressure from his client to complete it. I gave him a window of my availability from 1:30-3:00 that afternoon. He got back to me with the contract at 3:30, indicating he knew he had blown my window, but asking if I could review it "ASAP." Since the holiday fell on a weekend, everyone had Monday off as the official holiday. I was intending to spend Friday evening to Monday night in various family get togethers, including grocery-shopping and meal preparation for same.

This is an important client, and I have difficulty saying no to him. He is an authority figure for me. One of my character defects is people-pleasing, even when it compromises my self-care.

My pre-recovery self would have resentfully gotten up at 4 am on Saturday to work on the contract. Instead, I emailed the client on Friday, asking if anyone on his end would be available to review my input before Tuesday. He responded saying that indeed, it could wait until Tuesday. I had the contract to him 9:30 am on Tuesday, and felt proud of my boundaries and sticking up for myself. My happy client got back to me on Wednesday, thanking me for my good work.

Meditation December 24

I think meditation is particularly hard for work addicts. My whole addiction is about being unable to stop and just be. I'm a "human doing," rather than a "human being." There is a constant craving for more stimulation, something to react to. Just being is just boring. Surely someone has emailed me or I need to return a message? Yet meditation asks me to do the most painful thing possible: to stop the stimulation for a moment or two. I think I'm going to die.

I try lots of different ways to meditate. Focus on breathing, sounds, relaxing parts of my body in succession, written meditation. I worked up from a moment to five minutes to ten minutes a day to half an hour. On Sundays, I go to a meditation class where we practice and/or discuss various methods of meditation and our experience with them. I even attended a weekend retreat to hear teachings on meditation, and a weeklong silent meditation retreat.

The 11th step asks me to seek to improve my conscious contact with my Higher Power. Investigating and trying new ways to meditate is my way of improving that relationship, trying to keep it fresh because it inevitably gets stale. The 3rd step asks me to surrender my will and my life to my Higher Power. Giving my HP a chance to get a word in edgewise about his will for me seems like a reasonable step in the direction of turning my will over to him.

Prayer and Meditation December 25

"A daily contemplative practice is something we might formally adopt even prior to reaching Step Eleven. Before accepting any new commitments, we ask a Higher Power for guidance. For many of us, being still and sitting quietly are difficult and painful at first. The practice of letting go of the constant chatter in our heads can however lead to a gradually evolving peace of mind. This serenity is a soothing, healing contrast to the excitement, rush, and pleasurable intensity we have sought through our compulsive busyness and constant worry. Meditation lets us experience ourselves insulated from the resentments and fears that drive workaholism and work avoidance. Renewed, we are able to move back into our daily lives in a balanced way." –The Workaholics Anonymous Book of Recovery, 2nd Edition

My sponsor encouraged me to pray and meditate from my first days in recovery. Even after thirteen years, I still get down on my knees twice a day and remind myself that I'm not in charge. And meditation? Well, it is the anti-workaholic.

10th Step Inventory   December 26

I write a daily tenth step inventory about 95% of the time. This vacation week has been a struggle for me because my son is home from college, my family generally stays up later than me, and I don't want to miss out on the social time. Part of my recovery from work addiction is trying to get more fun into my day. Hanging out with my family is fun. But I'm also "supposed" to do a 10th step inventory and get enough sleep. Recovery tells me "Even when offered the best, say no if you need the rest." I can get rigid and perfectionistic about working my steps. It's hard to strike the right balance between step work and fun, when they seem to conflict with each other.

My 10th step inventory tracks the AA Big Book questions, and I've also incorporated some questions customized to my character defects and generally call me out on my shit. Ironically, one of the questions I ask myself in my 10th step is "What did I do today for fun and inactivity?"

I try to reconcile it this way: vacation is an anomaly in my year. I have to compromise sometimes on vacation: I can't eat my usual foods, go to my usual meetings, workout in the same ways. But vacation is a small percentage of my year. What I do the vast majority of the year is what really makes or breaks my program and life. So, it's ok to cut some corners on vacation, as long as I get back into my routine when vacation is over.

Project Management   December 27

I called my sponsor in a panic over three projects looming in front of me. How would I ever be able to get them done? I had two work conferences and one personal project—decorating my bedroom. I was most fearful my bedroom would never get done. A project like that— one without a deadline—is the most problematic for me. I could imagine it languishing for years because I often put myself last. It all felt hopeless.

My sponsor helped me to break the process down. The first work conference would be in March. I needed to make arrangements to set

223

up 10 meetings at the conference. I could start working on those logistics in February.

The second work conference was in May. I needed to set up 16 meetings there and, because everyone's calendar for that event fills up early, I needed to start working on those in March.

That left January for me to work on the bedroom. I made a list of the tasks involved: paint the walls, pick out carpeting and have it installed, buy furniture, buy wall hangings, and have someone hang the artwork. I assigned one task to each week in January. It really helped me to focus on first things first. Whenever one of the later-dated projects entered my mind, I told myself, "Now is not your time, I'll worry about you next week, or whenever." So then I was free to just do the single task I assigned to myself by Friday. How liberating!

I completed the bedroom by the end of January and it was beautiful. I set up the conference meetings and they came off without a hitch. These are skills I didn't possess before recovery.

Service and Humility   December 28

Step 12 calls on me to be of service to others. It was new to me in recovery to offer service to others and ask nothing in return. I'm used to being paid top dollar for my time as an attorney. But we do 12th Step work "for fun and for free." Luckily, I've had great examples of many women who offered their time and experience to me without wanting anything in return. Now, I'm just passing along what I freely received.

My ego sometimes intruded on sponsee relationships. I felt disrespected when they didn't show up. I wondered why my sponsees thought they didn't need to work as hard as me to get the "cash and prizes." I got relief from this as I went along, through many painful inventories and surrenders. Thankfully, it has now been years since I've needed to inventory a sponsee situation.

And I'm grateful for the lessons learned from sponsees. Anytime I experience humility is good. I didn't have much before recovery. It is still an effort not to take credit for my situation today—my recovery, my brains, my marriage, my kids, my house, my job. Fact is, I wouldn't have any of it if I hadn't gotten help from others and God in this program.

I ask God every morning in my prayers to help me to not take credit for the miracles he has brought about in my life.

Preserving Energy   December 29

I seem to have loads of energy early in the day and progressively less as the day goes on. Because of this, I can foolishly squander energy in the morning because it feels so abundant, and then I am exhausted later. Recently, I had to go downtown for three business meetings. I also had a sponsee meeting at my home later in the afternoon, as well as a 12-Step meeting in the evening. I could take any one of various methods of transportation downtown: drive, train or rideshare. In the past, I would have taken the train and walked a long distance on both ends of the train ride. This is certainly the least expensive way to commute. But, keeping in mind my rather overly-ambitious schedule, I decided to take a rideshare instead. I made it to my first meeting refreshed and ready. My next meeting was across town. Again, I could have walked for half an hour. I am always trying to fit more exercise into my days. Instead, I took a cab, and arrived fresh and with enough time to find a restroom before my meeting. That one too went well.

Finally, my lunch meeting was across town yet again. I had half an hour and could have walked, but I opted again for a cab and arrived fresh and ready to impress. That meeting also went great.

This is new behavior for me. I always want to crunch as much as I can into my day without regard for my physical and mental resources. It feels good to pamper myself when circumstances call for it. This was an unusually busy day. Anything I could do to make it gentler on myself was the right action. Other days and circumstances will call for choosing the less expensive route or the one that provides more exercise. This day wasn't it.

Sponsorship   December 30

More than any other addiction, workaholism is cunning in the way it convinces me I'm not a work and activity addict. I need constant reminding.

Sponsoring others has been integral in helping me out of my denial. Not only am I regularly meeting with sponsees to do stepwork, but they are calling me to discuss their latest work addiction manifestation. This helps keep my work addiction at the forefront of my brain.

Due to the lack of sponsors in work addiction programs, much of my sponsorship has been long distance, so we rely heavily on the phone. I have each sponsee write answers to the questions in the WA Book of Recovery. When she finishes each step, we set up a time to talk. She reads her answers to me and I read my answers to her. Hearing other workaholics' specific experiences as generated by the questions is enormously helpful to me. I am amazed at the thoughtfulness and thoroughness of the answers. Reading my own answers, written a few years back now, brings me face to face again with my powerlessness over this disease. The entire experience of sharing our similar acting out and thinking processes helps us bond.

I don't call my sponsees to check up on them. I don't treat them like they are my friends, although we are friendly with one another. I need to stay detached from the relationship in order to be of maximum usefulness to them.

So far, the only reasons I might terminate a sponsee relationship is if she treats me disrespectfully or she won't do any stepwork. I don't require sponsees to work the steps in any time period, or to do service, although I strongly encourage them to do service to give back what they are receiving from the recovery community. So far, I haven't had to terminate a sponsee relationship, although sponsees do leave me from time to time.

Overall, sponsoring women has been an amazing tool in my toolkit for combatting work and activity addiction. There's nothing like getting a call from a fellow work addict when I'm right in the middle of working on something intensely, and surrendering to my HP by picking up the call to get out of my head for a few minutes.

Retreat   December 31

For many years now in recovery, I have been able to go to a 12-Step retreat after Christmas. It is usually Dec 29-Jan 1. Just three-four days. I take a break from the shopping, wrapping, baking, cleaning, decorating and family visiting. The retreat is at this amazing rustic log cabin-like center, all decorated for the holidays with a constant fire going in the big meeting room. We have spiritual services, yoga, 12-Step meetings, healthy meals together, games, long walks, and bonfires outside by the frozen lake. Lots of time for fellowship, step work and in some years, writing this book. It is a time for reflection backward and forward. But mostly, it is a retreat from my to-do list which seems to control me during December.

"If I settle for my wildest dreams, I will be selling myself short."
–   overheard at a WA meeting

Index

Topic	Day
12 Step Recovery	Mar 18, Mar 19, Mar 25, Apr 9, Apr 19, May 27, Sep 9, Sep 12, Nov 7
20 Questions	Sep 6
80-hour Work Week	May 22, Jul 24
AA Big Book	Feb 8, Feb 25, Oct 5
Abstinence Date	Jan 15
Abundance	Oct 7
Acceptance	Jan 16, Jan 19, Feb 6, Apr 7, May 14, Jun 2, Jun 30, Aug 14, Oct 26, Nov 16, Nov 29, Dec 4, Dec 18
Accepting Help	Apr 25
Accountability	Sep 27
Acting "As if"	Feb 10, Jul 12, Aug 13, Oct 28, Nov 7
Acting Out	Apr 19, Jul 10
Action Plan	Jan 4, Jan 28, May 6, July 6, July 11, Jul 22, Aug 6, Aug 23, Sep 20, Sep 21, Oct 11, Oct 16, Oct 23, Oct 30, Nov 29, Dec 3, Dec 5, Dec 22
Activism	Jan 26, Feb 6
Activity chart	Jan 7, Apr 26
Addiction	Mar 24, Jul 28
Adrenalizing	Mar 6, Mar 20, Apr 20, May 20, Jun 27, Aug 20, Nov 13
Affirmations	Jan 11, Feb 28, Mar 4, May 28, Apr 4, Apr 22, Apr 24, May 4, May 30, Jun 4, Jul 4, Aug 2, Sep 4, Sep 18, Nov 2, Dec 2

228

Topic	Day
Alcohol	May 14, Jul 16
Ambition	Jan 3, Feb 26, Mar 26, Apr 6, Apr 19, Sep 25, Oct 9, Nov 8
Amends	Mar 8, Apr 12, Apr 17, Apr 21, Jul 30, Aug 18, Sep 5, Sep 17, Sep 28, Oct 3, Oct 13, Nov 25, Dec 6
Amends to self	Jan 29
Anger	Mar 22, Jun 16, Sep 15, Oct 19, Oct 20, Dec 1
Anorexia	Oct 22
Anxiety	Jan 4, Apr 29, May 10, May 28, Jun 8, Aug 6, Sep 2, Oct 11, Oct 28, Nov 4, Nov 6, Dec 8
Anxiety, Morning	Jan 20, May 10, Nov 4
Appearances	Sep 8
Approval-seeking	May 14, Sep 27, Oct 10, Nov 13
Asking for Help	Jan 19, Apr 25, Jul 24, Jul 31, Aug 11, Sep 22
Attention	Apr 24, Jul 14
Attitude about Work	Feb 14
Authority Figures	Feb 5, Feb 7, Apr 24, Jun 20, Sep 8, Nov 11, Nov 13, Dec 23
Awareness	Oct 8
Babies	Aug 10
Balance	Feb 22, Sep 30, Dec 17
Bathroom breaks	Jan 4, Apr 20, Jun 9, Jun 27, Nov 29,
Being Enough	Apr 4
Being where I am	May 19, Oct 16

Topic	Day
Being Wrong	Apr 5, May 7, Jun 26
Beliefs	Apr 3
Betrayal	Mar 22
Better Than	Jun 14
Binging	May 27, Nov 26, Dec 10
Body	Nov 24
Bookending	Aug 23
Bosses	Mar 8, Jul 14
Bottom Lines	Jan 15, Jan 25, Mar 18, Jun 16, Jun 22, Jul 27, Dec 11, Dec 14
Boundaries	Jan 10, Jul 8, Nov 9, Dec 19, Dec 23
Brainstorming	Oct 24
Broccoli tasks	Jul 3
Calculating	Apr 16
Capable	May 30
Careers	Dec 17
Care-taking	Dec 19
Carrying the Message	Dec 9
Catastrophizing	Nov 3
Character Defects	Feb 20, Feb 28, Mar 4, Mar 28, Apr 11, Apr 24, May 9, Jun 4, Jun 28, Jul 4, Jul 29, Aug 2, Aug 26, Sep 4, Sep 8, Sep 16, Sep 27, Nov 2, Nov 16, Nov 28, Nov 30, Dec 2
Change	Feb 27
Changing Careers	May 11
Checking messages	Mar 18, Sep 12
Clients	Sep 26
Choices	Feb 19, Nov 30

Topic	Day
Dancing	Nov 24, Dec 20
Decisiveness	Feb 19, Mar 10
Delegation	Jan 1, Jan 19, Feb 3, Mar 20, Jul 19, Jul 22, Sep 12, Nov 12, Nov 13
Denial	Mar 16, Jul 24, Sep 12
Dependence	Jul 8
Depression	May 14, Aug 6, Sep 2, Nov 7
Detachment	Aug 11
Diagnosing Work Addiction	Apr 7
Difficult People	Aug 25, Sep 26
Dishonesty	Jul 2, Aug 4, Aug 12, Sep 28, Nov 15, Nov 30
Dogs	Aug 10
Drama	Feb 28, Mar 6, Jul 30, Sep 28
Drinking	Jan 1
Drugs	Sep 2
Eating	Jun 29
Ego	Feb 23, Feb 24, Apr 6, Apr 12, Apr 14, Jun 10, Jul 30, Aug 14, Aug 24, Sep 24, Sep 28, Oct 20, Dec 1, Dec 28
E-mail	Jan 1, Mar 3, Mar 12, Mar 17, Mar 18, Jun 16, Jun 17, Jun 22, Jul 20, Aug 31, Sep 26, Oct 30, Dec 10
Embarrassment	Oct 12
Embezzling	Sep 5, Nov 15
Emotional Intimacy	Feb 18, Sep 4
Emotional Security	May 28, Aug 4, Oct 19
Emotional Sobriety	May 14

Topic	Day
Holidays	Nov 27
Honesty	Jan 19, Feb 26, Apr 9, Apr 10, Apr 11, Apr 12, Apr 13, Apr 14, Apr 15, Oct 2, Nov 5, Nov 15
Hope	Mar 14, Aug 28, Oct 30
Hopelessness	Nov 7
How it Was	Sep 12
Humiliation	Oct 12
Humility	Feb 17, Feb 24, Mar 8, Apr 12, May 1, May 3, Jun 14, Aug 14, Oct 12, Oct 14, Dec 1, Dec 28
Humor	Jan 1, Sep 12
Hunger	May 20
Hurrying	Jun 27, Dec 4
IALAC	May 30
Indecision	Feb 19, Mar 30
"I" Statements	Feb 9, Oct 2, Dec 14
Identity = Profession	Jun 13
Illness	Jan 22, Nov 18
Illusion of Control	Jul 18
Image Management	Feb 20, Apr 6, Apr 21, May 13, Jun 10, Aug 24, Sep 24
Impatience	Nov 16
Inactivity	Apr 18
Inferiority	Jun 14
Injustice	Sep 28
Insanity	Feb 23, Mar 2, May 2, Jun 2, Jun 5, Jun 27, Jul 23, Jul 30, Jul 31, Aug 3, Sep 1, Sep 30, Oct 31, Nov

Topic	Day
	Oct 19, Nov 2
Loveable	May 30
Loving Kindness	Dec 8
Lying	Apr 17, May 3, Oct 20, Nov 15
Management	Aug 16
Manipulation	Jul 30
Martyrdom	Nov 17
Massage	Nov 24
Matching Energy	Jun 30
Media	Jan 26, Feb 16, Apr 27, Jun 25, Sep 4
Meditation	Jan 9, Jan 18, Jan 20, Feb 6, Feb 12, Feb 16, Mar 20, Mar 29, Apr 23, May 12, Jun 1, Jun 3, Jul 1, Jul 13, Jul 23, Jul 26, Aug 1, Sep 20, Oct 4, Oct 17, Oct 23, Nov 4, Nov 7, Nov 24, Nov 29, Dec 4, Dec 24, Dec 25
Meetings	Jan 18, Feb 11, Mar 14, Apr 28, May 24, Aug 3, Aug 23, Sep 12, Oct 23, Nov 12, Nov 24, Nov 25, Dec 14
Mental Illness	Jul 8, Aug 25
Merton Prayer	Sep 11
Minding my Own Business	Aug 15
Mistakes	Mar 4, Apr 17, May 4, Jun 15, Jun 26, Sep 24, Nov 5, Nov 11, Nov 15
Moment of Silence	Oct 15

241

Topic	Day
	12, Jun 16, Jun 19, Jun 30, Jul 17, Sep 1, Sep 15, Oct 17, Nov 15, Nov 22, Dec 1, Dec 11, Dec 14, Dec 17, Dec 27, Dec 28, Dec 30
Staff	Feb 27, Jun 17
Standing up for Myself	Jun 20, Oct 27, Dec 21, Dec 23
Starfish Story	Feb 6
Status	Aug 29
Step 1	Jan 1, Apr 9, Apr 30
Step 2	Jan 12, Feb 2, Mar 2, Mar 21, Apr 2, Apr 9, Apr 30, May 2, Jun 2, Jul 23, Jul 31, Aug 3, Aug 13, Aug 31, Sep 1, Sep 30, Oct 1, Oct 31, Nov 1, Nov 20
Step 3	Feb 8, Mar 9, Mar 14, Apr 9, Apr 30, Oct 10, Dec 18
Step 4	Feb 25, Apr 1, Apr 10, Jul 8, Aug 4, Aug 12, Sep 8, Sep 15, Oct 6, Oct 12, Oct 13, Oct 19, Nov 3, Nov 30
Step 5	Feb 18, Apr 10, May 1, Nov 15
Step 6	Jan 9, Jan 11, Feb 28, Apr 11, May 4, Jun 4, Sep 18, Nov 2, Nov 28, Dec 2
Step 7	Jan 31, Apr 11, Jul 29, Nov 28
Step 8	Apr 12, Apr 21, May 3, Sep 5, Oct 3, Oct 13
Step 9	Apr 12, Apr 17, Nov 15, Dec 6
Step 10	Jan 24, Apr 13, May 3, May 17,

Acknowledgement

I would like to thank Lee Inkmann for her editing skills, my sponsor for her regular cheerleading and encouragement, and my husband for putting up with me through this process.

Made in the USA
Middletown, DE
14 October 2021